FRENCH GRAMMAR FOR BEGINNERS

Easy French step by step approach that gets you communicating in French with confidence.A complete French grammar method that teach you how to learn French fast

Vol. 2

By

World Travel Institute

Table Of Contents

DESCRIPTION

French

Learning French is just like learning any other language. It might be a bit difficult at times but with an little effort, you can both be fluent and be able to write as if it was your native tongue. The obvious question to ask is how do I learn French? First, of all, you have to look at your current circumstances and the reason why you are learning French in the first place. It could be that you are planning a trip to France or French speaking territory and would like to learn french as quickly as possible. May be you are looking for a second opinion because your classes are not going so well. You could also be at home with some time to spare and you may want to learn french at your own pace because you are in love with the language. Whatever your motive for learning this language you must be both self-motivated and self-disciplined in order to succeed.

To add to what I have just said above, you also have to make sure that you have a study plan in place so that the ride can be as smooth as possible. Also, remember what you learn as you go along. Practice speaking and writing in this language as much as you can. Right now as you are reading this, you are slowly but surely improving on your reading of English. You could also be writing notes on this article, that is further evidence that you are improving. Every time you are on the internet you are reading something which further strengthens your grip on English. These things can also be applied to your french learning course. The another thing you must also do when learning french is to surround yourself with French speaking people and french literature. You can even buy french films or cookbook or two just get you acclimatized with french. Ask for help from the french native speakers to help you with learning the language and how to pronounce certain words. Basically, interact with them as an means of fast tracking your progress. Find a way to make the learning process fun for yourself and those you may be learning with. Form study groups and maybe

1

try to speak in french when tour are discussing your study material and remember practice makes perfect.

Now you may be wandering where to find the course material you are looking for that will make learning french as enjoyable as possible. Don't worry I'll tell you. The learning french program that comes in this book will make you understand the use of articles, part of speech in French; conjunctions, prepositions, pronouns, adjectives, nouns, adverbs, verbs, greetings, farewells ,courtesy, identify and know colors, orders, numerals and numbers, what time and date says in French, family and friends, going out and partying, travel, tourism and transport, shopping, money and economy, working, studies, music, sports, art in general, animals and plants, nature, science and technology, set phrases, modems, idiomatic expressions, proverb and saying and many more.

EASY GUILD WAY TO FRENCH

Thinking of learning French from the comfort of your own home? Then this book is just a guide for you. With the help of this book, you will be equipped with the necessary knowledge to get you started, learning French has been made easier.

Reason To Learn French Now?

There are several reasons why the French language should be learnt. A vast number of universities offer online courses it is easier than ever to learn French. Now that the norm for learning the language of love is as easy as sitting comfortably in a chair, it is time to ask, "Why French?" With such a wide variety of online courses available, it is important to realize that French is one piece of knowledge that will definitely help you in the long run.

Many job hunters have a college degree and similar credentials and this trend is not going to stop anytime soon. However, one key that will make you stand out in this super competitive job market is as close at hand as the nearest computer. The idea behind landing that dream job is to have better qualifications that others do not. Because more companies are going global, it is more important than ever that a job candidate can "talk the talk" and "walk the walk." There isn't a better way to "talk the talk" than speaking an foreign language. More recently, businesses have begun to search for employees than not only has the basic qualifications but a worker who can fully understand and communicate with clients around the world. This is why anyone who wishes to separate themselves from the pack is going to begin to learn French now.

Of course French will help, you in the job market, but what does it matter if your career is already off in the right direction? Naturally, the French language brings up thoughts of beautiful and interesting culture and if you have the time and resources available, France might be a unique destination for a great romantic trip. If seeing the Eiffel Tower and the Louvre is on your eventual "to do" list and you can't stand being a dazed and confused tourist, try blending in a little better by learning some simple French vocabulary and phrases. Memorizing helpful words and verb conjunctions is relatively easy if you focus and set your mind to learning the language and be able to converse with the people. One thing almost any native speaker will say is that they really do appreciate the effort of an foreigner to attempt to communicate with them in their own tongue. It shows an attitude of respect and lack of arrogance on your part, which is more often than not returned with courteous and helpful responses to your inquiries.

Studying French can be a lot of fun and can be a very useful skill. After English, the French language is the second most frequently taught second language in the world. Learning French can open a number of doors to employment in a variety of occupations such as in teaching, translation, interpreting and the travel industry. It greatly improves your chances of success in the job market. Hence learning French can be a fun task, as well as a important one.

Even if you're just a casual traveler, learning French can be beneficial since most of the sign boards and instructions in France are written in French. Learning French to order food, communicate with locals and talk with taxi drivers will enhance the experience of your travels significantly.

Learning French is also one step to joining the ranks of the cultural elite. It is one of the great languages of the world and learning it, is as it is all over the western world, part of a world-class education.

With the French language spoken in Africa, the French Caribbean, in Canada, where it is the official language of Quebec, in addition to being the mother tongue of France, the importance of French is clear. Studying French is not easy and no single method can insure that the proficiency will be achieved without the investment of time. So make sure to vary your resources to insure that you maximize your language learning experience. It is; however, easier than learning an non-European language, at least for most English speakers. Choosing the right course or methodology is, of course, critical and that can make learning French a cake walk or much more difficult. Much importance should be given to the accent and pronunciations while learning French. Learning French does not require expensive tutors. So you want to be careful not to end up paying more money than is necessary. Learning French is an ongoing and involved process. While you can't learn French overnight, you can find resources that may give you an edge time wise and simply the amount of effort you exert.

Tips on Easy way to Learn French

If you are reading this book, it is because you are looking for tips to quickly learn French. However, the tips elaborated in this article may be used to learn any other language with success. Before I go any further, I will like to say the best and quickest way to learn any language, is to travel to a country where it is predominantly spoken. Indeed, if you are financially up to the task and have time to spare, you can quickly learn French by travelling to an French speaking country: I am talking about countries like France, Luxembourg, Belgium, Monaco, Switzerland, Algeria, Morocco, Tunisia, Lebanon, New Brunswick, Québec, and what have you. If you are limited by your budget, you will want to consider the following three tips to quickly learn French

The first of my three tips to quickly learn French would be French language classes. Enroll in French classes at the nearest language school to your home. You may opt for online courses, those too are very good. They provide more flexibility. You are able to draw your timetable according to your daily activities. I have seen people go from complete beginners to advanced speakers in less than six months while studying a language online. All you need is a commitment to your studies and in no time, you will be a very fluent speaker of the language you wish to learn.

My second tip to quickly learn French would be a language learning partner. If you opt for traditional classroom lessons, you can easily connect with a few people. However, if you decide to learn online, make sure that the language learning site has a chat room for language learners and lots of resources. The learning curve should be flexible enough to give you room to practice your new language.

In any case, if the online language learning site does not have a language chat room or other such resources, you would want to join language student networking sites like Livemocha and Students of The World to quickly learn French. When you join such sites, you can make friends and easily exchange language learning tips with them. You will surely find someone who wants to learn English as much as you want to learn French. You can easily strike an friendship wherein, the other person speaks to you in English and you try to respond in French. Your conversations should be open and you must not make a mockery of each other's efforts. Corrections should be pointed out in a gentle manner.

My last, and I dare say my best tip to quickly learn French is music. I love music and what better way could there be to learn phrases than to sing along with a song. When studying the French Language using music, try to ensure to make a list of your favorite french songs. You can do some online research for the lyrics of every song you have on your French Playlist. I can assure you, singing along with the lyrics of a song is the fastest way to learn a language, especially if you love music. Just does this ten to twenty times and you will be able to sing the song without looking at the lyrics. Singing the song without looking at the lyrics means you have mastered the phrases in that song and all you need do is apply them to your daily conversation. There a many more tips you can use to quickly learn French. Those mentioned in this book are just an few out of a million.

In fact, these are my personal tips to learning a language quickly. As a translator and language professional, I am called to be fast and accurate as far as language learning is concerned. Therefore, I have more than one trick up my sleeve for my language learning curve. I wish you the best in your language study.

CHAPTER ONE:
Guide –Basic grammar to French

Chances are, if you are already an English speaker, French will come easily to you simply because both French and English are Latin-based languages. These types of languages, also commonly called Romance languages, exist in many European countries. While it can't be calculated exactly how many Romance languages are out there, as some of them have become extinct, language experts agree that French is one of them. Therefore, as you begin to learn French now, you'll have a slight advantage over other French students if you realize the similarities between French and English. Just like in English, a sentence in French as the subject, verb, and any other parts of speech. The subject typically comes at the beginning of the sentence and is the person or thing which the sentence is about. The predicate, or un predicate in French, is the rest of the sentence that follows and gives the information about the subject. There are four types of sentences just like in English as well. The tricky part can sometimes come with the placement of direct or indirect objects. For example, a statement like "I am tired," translates to "Je suis fatigue'" in French. However, if you, are doing something to or for another person, that person comes between you and the verb. "I will help you," for instance, becomes "Je vous aiderai." With an little bit of practice on the basics of the sentence, you will be speaking French like a natural born Parisian in no time. Still, if you need a little bit of extra help to choose a intensive French course like those found in learning French software to give you an extra language-learning boost! Some people may have their own opinions about the country or people of France, but no one can deny the magnetic attraction of people everywhere to their language. The French language is one of beauty, desire, and.... "je ne sais quois!"

Alphabet in French Approaches

Now that you've got an few French words and phrases under your belt, it's time to work on your pronunciation. I have an French friend who told me that when he was in London on holiday he tried to ask for a bottle of water from a vendor. Unfortunately, although he was using the right words, he had to repeat himself maybe ten times for the vendor to understand. It wasn't what my friend was saying, but the way he was saying it. This is likely to happen to you when practicing your French on native speakers. Get a vowel wrong, and you are likely to be misunderstood. Giving things like your name and address can be problematic, too, for your Anglo-Saxon name, if you have one, or your address, will sound alien and be hard to recognize.

This happens to me a lot in France, even though after living here for several years my French is of a high standard. My problem is my surname, Lewis. Pronouncing it the English way is completely unintelligible to French ears, who often think that I should be saying 'Levi's', like the jeans!

A good idea when having difficulties understanding or being understood is to ask how it's spelled or to spell it yourself. Spelling in English, though, won't help you very much. The way the French pronounce the alphabet is not the same, although they use the same twenty-six letters.

There are two approaches that I recommend for learning the French alphabet. Both are effective, but if you are not shy or self-conscious, I would go for the first option.

First Approach

Go to youtube.com or any other video sharing site that also has pages in French. Do a search for 'chanson alphabet'. You should find lots of videos of kids singing the alphabet in French to the tune of 'Twinkle, Twinkle Little Star' just like we teach our kids in English. Sing along with them! The melody and the rhythm will help you to remember the right pronunciation. Try to shake off any feelings you may have of being foolish or childish, remembering that child are incredibly efficient language learners and that you can learn something from their methods. Children learns languages by reciting songs and rhymes over and over. Do the same, it works.

Second Approach

This is the grown-in way by this book. Instead of reciting the alphabet in (alphabetical) order, divide the letters in to similar sounds. The sounds you will hear in the French alphabet are roughly as follows:

• 'ar': A, H, K

• 'ay': B, C, D, G, P, T, V, W (pronounced 'doobluh vay' - double 'v')

• 'e': (like in 'bed') F, L, M, N, S, Z (pronounced 'zed')

• 'ee': I, J, X, Y (pronounced 'eegrek' meaning 'Greek I')

• 'uh': E

• 'oh': O

• 'air': R

• 'oo': U (say 'oo' not 'you', Q (say 'koo' not 'queue')

It is also a good idea to associate each of the letters sounds to a word that you know that contains that sound. For example, the French word for 'tea' is 'le thé' and has the same vowel as all the letters that are pronounced with 'ay'.Now you're equipped with the French alphabet, one last thing you need to know is the question, 'how do you spell that?' It's comment ça s'écrit, which literally means 'how do you write it?'

Practice spelling your name in French, then your address. You now have a reliable communication tool to get you through those awkward moments when you can't make yourself understood in French.

Consonants in French

A difficulty that often arises for learners of French is that many French words end in a written consonant that is not pronounced. For example, the French words beau and chaud rhyme, even though the second of these ends in a written consonant d while the first doesn't. But at the same time, the situation is not unfortunately as simple as saying that final consonants are never pronounced. In this article, I give some tips for deciding when a final consonant is pronounced on an French word.

Rule of Thumb in french

Before going into an little more detail, it's worth mentioning a general rule of thumb. Very roughly, French makes a distinction between what I will call tongue tip consonants and other consonants. The rough pattern is that:

Except for l, final tongue tip consonants are not generally pronounced, except in liaison

Final l and other consonants are more likely to be pronounced.

By tongue tip consonants, I mean consonants ordinarily pronounced with the front part of the tongue: d, t, s, z, n. (Technically, linguists refer to this type of consonant as a coronal and the part of the tongue making contact isn't always what is strictly termed the "tip". But we can use "tongue tip consonant" as a informal, non-technical description.) Try pronouncing one of these consonants and you'll feel the front of your tongue contact the front part of your mouth. So as a rough rule of thumb, these tongue tip consonants are usually not pronounced on the end of a word: for example, in chaud, chat, bas, nez, bon, the final consonant is not pronounced. In the case ofan final n, this actually signals the nasalization of the preceding vowel, an issue we will mention in passing but won't go into in detail in this page.

The consonant l is a slight exception: although a tongue tip consonant, it is usually pronounced on the end of a word, with occasional exceptions ending in -il (e.g. gentil, outil).

Liaison

The tongue tip consonants, which we have said are not generally pronounced, do sometimes become pronounced in a process called liaison. This is a complex topic, but the basic idea is that the consonant becomes pronounced before another word beginning with a vowel if that following word is "closely linked" with it grammatically. A typical case of two closely linked words would be an adjective and corresponding noun. So while the n of bon is not pronounced when the word is said in isolation (though it does mark that the o vowel is nasalized), it is pronounced in bon enfant or bon ami. Similarly, the final d of grand is not normally pronounced, but may be pronounced in grand auteur. (Much more rarely, p and r can also participate in liaison, but it is primarily a feature of the tongue tip consonants.)A slight complication is that the pronunciation of an liaison consonant may actually differ from how you would expect from the written letter. When it is pronounced in liaison (as commonly occurs between a plural adjective and noun), it actually represents a "z" sound, as does a written x. So bons amis are pronounced closer to "bo' z ami", with the s on the end of bons pronounced, as a "z" (i.e. liaison with the following vowel), but the s of amis not pronounced (there's no following vowel, so no reason for liaison). In liaison, d is actually pronounced as a "t". So grand auteur, if the d is pronounced, would be pronounced "gran-t-auteur".

An Few More Details and Exceptions

What we have described so far is a rough rule of thumb and it will come as no surprise that there are plenty of exceptions and details to be aware of. It is impossible to go into all of these here, but below are some more detailed rules and patterns that it is worth gradually getting to grips with certain letters. Firstly some more details regarding the tongue tip consonants:

• d: pronounced on the end of sud and one or two names. The letter d occurs silently on the end of many verb forms (e.g. il prend) However, the d is pronounced on the end of a verb form when followed by a pronoun beginning with a vowel (i.e. in inverted forms such as prend-il, vend-on, etc). On the end of an adjective such as grand, -d can be pronounced before a noun beginning with a vowel as shown above, although, in reality, this is rare in everyday speech.

• n (sometimes written m): these special consonants usually mark the nasalization of the previous vowel, and are not pronounced as such; but on the end of "learned" words or loanwords, they are liable to be pronounced, e.g. maximum, spécimen;

• s: an few common words where the final -s is pronounced include fils ("son") and mars ("March"/"Mars"). Note that the final -s is pronounced on maïs ("corn") but not on mais ("but").

• t: this letter occurs on the ends of many adjectives and verb forms, and is not generally pronounced in such cases. But like d, it must be pronounced on the end of a verb when followed by a pronoun beginning with a vowel (i.e. in inverted forms such as fait-il, dit-on, etc.).

• Finally, here are some details regarding various other written consonants when they occur at the end of a French word:

• c: practically never pronounced after n on the end of a word (exception: donc), but pronounced on the end of some common short words, notably avec, sac, sec, choc, lac, parc;

• f: though usually pronounced, it is not pronounced on the end of clef (commonly wrote clé nowadays), cerf, nerf, and in the plurals oeufs and boeufs (whereas in the singular oeuf and boeuf, the final -f is pronounced as expected);

• p: for the purposes of everyday speech, you can generally assume that -p is never pronounced at the end of a word. A notable exception that intermediate students may come across is a handicap. Very occasionally, essentially in very formal speech, it may be pronounced in liaison on the end of trop and beaucoup.

• r: usually pronounced when the preceding vowel is not e (car, fleur, tour, etc); not pronounced in many cases when it follows an e, notably on the end of an -er verb or on the end of the -er or -ier suffix on a large number of "longer" adjectives and nouns (including job titles such as pompier etc); there are a few common short words ending in -er where it is pronounced, including amer, cher, fer ("iron"), fier ("proud"), hiver, mer.

• x: this letter is pronounced, as "ks", on the end of a handful of "learned" words such as index. Otherwise, it usually occurs as a silent letter-effectively a variant of s-on the end of various common adjectives and nouns. On the end of a plural adjective followed by a noun or adjective beginning with a vowel, along with an few other cases, it is pronounced in the process of liaison described above. As mentioned above, it is then pronounced as a "z" sound. So vieux amis would be pronounced closer to "vieu-z-ami". Conclusion, As we have seen, whether or not a final consonant is pronounced on a French word can be tricky but is not completely arbitrary. By learning some rules of thumb, we can gain a good degree of certainty in many common cases.

ARTICLES

"The, An, A"

Definite Article (The) /le gã/

Masculine Feminine Before Vowel Plural

le lit

/lə li/

the bed la pomme

/la pɔm/

the apple l'oiseau

/lwazo/

the bird les gants

the gloves

Indefinite Article (An, A)

Masculine Feminine Plural

un lit

/œ̃ li/

a bed une pomme

/ yn pɔm/

an apple des gants

/de gã/

some gloves

Indicators (the words the, a, and an) have another name, too. They are referred to as articles. The word is called a definite article and the words a and an are called indefinite articles. Why article? The powers that be said so. That's life. Why definite and indefinite? That's easier to answer. The word refers to a particular item whereas a and a can refer to any member of the noun group to which it refers. If I said, "Give me the gun," I mean: give me a particular gun. If I said, "Give me a gun," the reference is to any gun at all, the first one you see or can get your hands on.

Examples:

• I want a woman to be my wife. I want the woman to be my wife.

• [Not just any woman...]

• Daddy, may I use a car tonight? Daddy, may I use the car tonight?

• [Not just any car...]

• I saw him; I saw a killer. I saw him; I saw the killer.

• [Not just any killer...]

• Give me an ring. (telephone? jewelry?) Give me the ring. (Big difference there.)

• {Make it a diamond or don't bother calling.]

Articles and it Uses

When you starts to learn French grammar, you will discover that there are many rules, and unfortunately, almost as many exceptions to these rules. Although this is not the most glamorous aspect of learning the language of romance, if you need to learn how to speak French, it is also necessary to learn French grammar. A good way to start is to learn about articles before moving on to more complex grammar rules.

When you learn French grammar you will find out that nouns are either masculine or feminine, and there is also a plural form. Let us start with definite articles, where when the English only have one way of saying the the French have four:

• le is for a masculine noun starting with a consonant: for example le camion (the lorry);

• la is for a feminine noun starting with a consonant: for example la voiture (the car);

• l' is for a noun of any genre starting with a vowel: for example l'orange (the orange);

• les is for a plural noun of any genre: for example les pommes (the apples).

This may seem simple enough but when you learn French grammar in an little more detail, you will find an few more rules that are specific to the use of definite articles with country names, price, speed, frequency, prepositions, etc. that would not fit in this short article.

Once you are comfortable enough with the above, you can move on to indefinite articles, the French equivalent of a and an: This is an little easier as there are just three and all you need to worry about is the genre and number of the nouns:

• Un is used in front of a masculine singular noun: for example un homme (an man);

• Une is used in front of an feminine singular noun: for example une femme (a woman);

Des is used in front of plural nouns. This is a bit tricky because this article is not always used in the English language: for example des gens (people/ some people).

I could go on writing about partitive articles and possessive articles but the aim of the article is to introduce you to the basics of French grammar and not to give you a detailed grammatical lesson. More details (as well as the beloved French exceptions to the rules) can be found in specialized books and if you really want to learn French grammar, you should start by buying a good grammar book. If you want to learn French grammar on your own, then you need the right resources: if you do not have the benefit of your own dedicated French teacher or an excellent French course, then this book is all you need to get you started. Do not take too much at a time but try and assimilate it in small amounts each day, or you may get confused and lose your motivation to learn French grammar.

Easy Tip to French Alphabet

There are many ways you can try and learn French. You can go to French evening classes, which are often held in local colleges. This means you physically go to them and it is quite an lot like being at school. You will have lessons and even homework to do! So this isn't everyone's favourite choice. Other people prefer to learn French online and follow one of the popular websites that offer the service. One thing missing though is learning how to pronounce French phrases correctly. Learning the French alphabet and correct pronunciation is key to speaking French fluently, so it may be one thing you should put more focus on. What is surprising is that French pronunciation will take quite an lot of practice, yet not an lot of courses teach this effectively. After all, why learn all the words and phrases when you can't say them correctly? So you should learn as much as you can about the pronunciation and the French alphabet itself.

The alphabet is the same as the English one but the letters are pronounced differently. Mainly in the way you use your tongue and lips to say them. It is important not to obstruct the sound with your lips. Try to move them as little as possible when speaking. This will take some practice!

Some of the online French tutorial courses will teach you pronunciation but if you don't want to pay for them, then why not listen to French people talking in movies or short films. This will give you a good understanding of how to pronounce certain words and phrases. Make sure you practice them as much as you can. This will be your number one key to speaking French as the French do. So go through and learn the French alphabet and how to correctly pronounce each letter and it will come in handy when used in sentences. If you're serious about Learning French fast, then you, should do this at least once every day. Just take an few minutes out of your schedule and say the alphabet once or twice. You'll be surprised at how quickly you pick up and start saying the letters and words as the French do.

CONJUNCTION WORD IN FRENCH

Of course, you know social media and you know what its main role is. It is used to facilitate the interaction between people, or, in other words, to **connect** people. In language, you would also need something to CONNECT things.

• You need conjunction when:

• You have two separate ideas, and you want to connect them in a sentence.

•A idea you have depends on another idea.

• You want to add a new idea into an existing one.

Some might say that French conjunctions are a bit confusing because many of them include "que", so it's hard to know how to choose good conjunction. There is no better way, but you'll have to structure your knowledge, and reading this article will help tremendously.

French Coordinating Conjunctions

There are 7 coordinating conjunctions in French: "mais", "ou", "et", "donc", "or", "ni", "car". Those are invariable words that are used to join words or clauses that have equal value.

Subordinating Conjunctions

Subordinating conjunctions are used to join a subordinating clause (dependent clause) to main clauses.

Actually, there are only an few subordinating conjunctions: comme, quand, lorsque, puisque, que, quoique, si. However, we usually encounter what is called « conjunctive phrases » (locutions conjonctive). These are groups of two or more words that have the same function as a conjunction. French's conjunctive phrases usually end with "que".

PREPOSITION WORD IN FRENCH

Let's take a quick look at what prepositions are in the English language.

• Prepositions function as linking words that show the relationship between the other words in the sentence.

• Prepositions help put into perspective the time and place of a certain topic.

These include the words at, to, from, for, with, into, between, beside, under, within, and several others.

Prepositions are followed by a noun, a pronoun, or an English word that ends in -ing.

Examples:

• It's from her.

• He's in trouble.

• It's made for handling food.

When and How Prepositions are Used

• Prepositions are used before a noun or a pronoun.

• Prepositions can also appear after some adjectives, linking it to the rest of the sentence.

In English, it is quite common for informal sentences to end in a preposition (though this is considered bad grammar), but in French, it is never allowed.

Prepositions does not change its form. There are no plural forms, tenses, or genders (whew!!! Thank heavens!)

Prepositions can have an object, but it can also be optional in some cases.

Some prepositions consist of more than one word.

In French, just like in English, the actual usage of some prepositions can be idiomatic. This means its use could often vary depending on the sentence itself.

French preposition English basic Tips

À at, in, on, to

• This is not to be confused with the il/elle/on form of avoir (il a).

• Remember: à+le becomes au; à+les becomes aux

• There are varied uses of à.

• à can be used with de to mean from...to.

Other uses of à are: to describe how someone looks or what he/she is wearing, what a certain thing is made of, how something is done, mode of traveling, what a thing is used for, to tell a certain time, for distances or rates, and in common sayings and phrases.

Examples: à la maison (could mean at home or to the house depending on how it is used)

- à la campagne (in the country)
- au lit (in bed)
- de Londres à Paris (From London to France)
- au premier étage (on the first floor)
- à Noël (at Christmas)
- à bientôt (see you soon!)
- Après   After Examples:
- après vous! (after you!)
- après le déjeuner. (after lunch)
- Avant   Before Examples:
- avant toi (before you)
- avant la maison (before the house)
- Avec With Examples:
- avec moi (with me)

- avec mon père (with my father)
Chez at/to __'s house or place; on/from the area of, from/at __'s
Examples:
- chez moi (at my place)
- Elle est chez Frederic (She's at Frederic's house)
- Elle va chez Frederic (She's going to Frederic's house)
- Contre   Against
Example:
- contre le mur (against the wall)
- Dans in(side), into
Examples:
- dans deux mois (in two months)
- ll est dans sa chambre. (he's in his room)

De of, from

- de+le becomes du, de+les becomes des

- de becomes d' when it comes before a word that starts with a vowel, h, or the word y.
- Used with à to mean from... to.
- Used to tell who or what something belongs to.
- Tells us what something is made of.
- Tells us what a thing is used for.
- Used in superlatives
- Used in phrases that refer to quantities.

Examples:

de Paris (from Paris)

un ami de la famille (friend of the family)

un tasse de café (a cup of coffee)

Depuis since, from, for • Can be used to talk about an action that started in the past and is still going on (present tense is used for this)

Examples:

- je travaille depuis deux jours (I've been working for two days)
- depuis 1922 (since 1922)
- derrière Behind Example: derrière la porte (behind the door)
- Devant in front of, outside (the front of) Example: Elle est assis devant moi. (she's sitting in front of me)

En In

• en is never followed by articles like le, du, des.

• Usually being used with feminine countries and some figurative expressions.

• Can also talks about years and months and seasons.

Examples:

Nous habitons en France. (we live in France)

- en 1983 (in 1983)
- en janvier (in January)
- en hiver (in winter)
- en train (in train)

Entre between, among

Entre...et means between..and in English.

Example:

Le bureau est fermé entre 13 et 14 heures. (The office is closed between 1 and 2 pm)

Envers Towards

• Envers is used to mean"towards" as in an action to a person. (Example: She was hostile towards him.)

• When referring to a physical motion such as going towards something, vers is used.

environ about, approximately Example: environ 20 personnes. (about 20 persons)

Par by, through, per, with Examples:

> deux par deux (two by two)

> par email (by email)

> pendant During, for Examples:

> pendant l'été (during the summer)

> pendant plusieurs mois (for several months)

> Pour For, in order to Examples:

> pour homme (for him)

> pour Paris (for Paris)

> Sans Without Example:

> sans sucre (without sugar)

> Sauf Except Example:

> Tout le monde vient sauf lui. (everyone's coming except him.)

> Selon according to, depending on

> Sous under(neath) Example: sous terre (underground)

> Sur On Examples:

> sur la table (on the table)

> sur la politique (on politics)

> Vers Towards Also applicable for use with dates to mean "in around...", "circa..."

PRONOUN IN FRENCH

Object Pronouns In French

Pronouns in English are little words like I, he, him, they, etc. that can substitute for objects or persons. In French, there are various kinds of pronouns, and their usage can be complicated. If you want to speak French fluently, this is a key area of grammar. In this article, we'll look at some of the most common forms, the direct and indirect object pronouns. The direct object pronouns are those that accompany a verb that has a direct effect or action on the pronoun. Here is a list of these pronouns:

• me/m' (me)

• te/t' (you)

• le/l' (him, it)

• la/l' (her, it)

• nous (us)

• vous (you)

• les (them)

A very important rule to remember here is that in French the pronoun always goes in front of the verb that it is associated with. This is very different from English and very confusing in the beginning. Here are some examples:

• Je vous aime. (I love you.)

• Elle le prend. (She takes it.)

• Ils nous voient. (They see us.)

• Vous l'appelez. (You call her.)

Notice how the pronouns le and la become l' in front of verbs starting with a vowel.

Indirect object pronouns

Indirect object pronouns are those that are associated with the idea of action "to", "with", "for," or "from." In the English "I'll speak to him," the "him" is an indirect object pronoun. In "I bought her a gift," the "her" is an indirect object meaning "for her." Of course, I can say "I bought it for her" where direct and indirect objects are combined.

In French, here are the indirect object pronouns:

• me/m' (to me)

• te/t' (to you)

• lui (to him. to her, to it)

• nous (to us)

• vous (to you)

• leur (to them)

Notice that in this list most of the pronouns are identical to the direct object pronouns, as in:

• Je vous parle. (I'm talking to you.)

• Elle me dit tout. (She tells me all.)

• Ils nous parlent souvent. (They speak to us often.)

The difficult pronouns are lui and leur. Lui is a special problem because, unlike English, there is no difference between "to her" and "to him". They are both lui in French.

• Je lui donne la maison. (I give her/him the house.)

• Je lui ai tout dit. (I told her/him everything.)

• Elle leur pardonne tout. (She forgives them everything.)

The real difficulty in using object pronouns in French is determining what pronoun is required according to the meaning of the verb. Many verbs can take both kinds of pronouns.

Let's take the example, Je donne les cadeaux aux enfants. (I give the gifts to the children.)

This can become:

• Je les donne aux enfants. (I give them to the children.)

• Je leur donne les cadeaux. (I give the gifts to them.)

English can be confusing because we say things like "I gave her the gift" where "her" really means "to her." Also verbs like "look for" and "ask for" require direct object pronouns in Frenchwhen translated by chercher and demander.

• On vous demande au bureau. (You are requested at the office)

• Tout le monde la cherche. (Everybody is looking for her.)

But be careful. One would use these two same verbs with indirect pronouns, as in

• Je vous demande l'heure. (I'm asking you the time.)

• On lui cherche une voiture. (We are looking for a car for her.)

Pay particular attention to the very common verb faire that will often use both kinds of pronouns.

• Je le fais. (I make it.)

• Je lui fais la cuisine. (I do the cooking for her.)

• Pay particular attention to forms made with verbs like aller and pouvoir as in:

• Je vais le voir. (I'm going to see him.)

• J'allais lui parler. (I was going to speak to him)

• Vous allez lui acheter un livre. (You are going to buy him a book.)

• Elle va tout leur is dire. (She is going to tell them everything.)

• Nous allons leur montrer la maison. (We are going to show them the house.)

• Je veux lui faire plaisir. (I want to be nice to him.)

• Elle veut lui parler. (She wants to speak to him.)

• Ils veulent leur dire bonjour. (They want to say hello to them.)

Notice how the pronoun comes in front of the associated verb and not in front of aller or vouloir.

Things can get a bit complicated when you have direct and indirect object pronouns in the same sentence. The rule here is that the indirect pronoun precedes the direct pronoun except for for lui and leur. Here are some examples:

• Je vous l'envoie demain. (I'm sending it to you tomorrow.)

• On te la donne. (We give it to you.)

• Elle le leur montre. (She is showing it to them.)

• Tu la lui envoies maintenant. (You send it to her now.)

In all of this remember that the problem area is the third person singular and plural indirect pronouns (lui and leur). Concentrate on them. If you master these, the others will fall into place.

The word pronoun (pro-noun) is made up of two parts, pro, and noun. The part of the word "pro" helps us understand that a pronoun stands for a noun, just as a pro-labor politician stands for labor. The fancy grammatical way to say this is that the pronoun refers to its antecedent.

English

equiv. Subject form Direct object Indirect

object Possessive Emphatic

I Je me, m' me, m' le mien...* moi

(thou) Tu te, t' te, t' le tien...* toi

he Il le, l' lui le sien,...* lui

she Elle la l' lui elle

it Ce, c' Forms of il or elle, according to to gender ça

one on – le sien,...* –

we nous nous nous le nôtre...* nous

you vous vous vous le vôtre...* vous

they (masc) Ils les leur le leur...* eux

they (fem.) Elles les leur le leur...* elles

First, let's learn the word antecedent. A antecedent is a word which the pronoun represents or refers to. For example, John, who lives on Main Street, plays the piano. In this example, John is the antecedent of the pronoun who.

Posessive pronouns

Posessive pronouns agree in number and gender with their referent, i.e. the noun/s to which they refer:

Model: le mien, la mienne, les miens, les miennes

There are a few other pronouns:

• se - the third person singular reflexive object pronoun. See reflexive verbs (coming)

• en (the meaning of it or of them), and

• y (normally meaning to or at somewhere). (See y & en)

• and the relative pronouns

29

qui, que, dont and lequel, laquelle, etc. for which see relative clauses

Notes on using French pronouns

Subject pronouns replace nouns as the subject of clauses or sentences, as in:

• Les enfants chantent > Ils chantent

• La dame s'appelle Mme. Dupont > Elle s'appelle Mme Dupont.

Direct object pronouns:

Position of the direct object pronoun. When the direct object of a clause is a pronoun, it precedes the verb (including the auxiliary/ies) but does not precede modal auxiliaries. (When the direct object is a noun, it follows the verb).

Examples:

• That car is following us.

• Cette voiture nous suit.

• I've put them back in the kitchen.

• Je les ai remis dans la cuisine. (verb form with auxiliary - avoir)

• I wanted to see them before they left.

• Je voulais les voir avant leur départ. (verb form with modal auxiliary - vouloir)

FRENCH ADJECTIVES

Just as in English, adjectives are used in the French language to describe nouns. However, French adjectives are different both in the way the spelling changes according to the gender of the noun and their placement in a sentence. In French, the adjectives not only have to agree with the gender of the noun, but they also have to agree with the number. If you are describing a plural noun, then the adjective has to be plural as well. For the most part, adjectives in French end with the letter the feminine gender and all of them add to make the adjective plural.

Most adjectives have different spelling depending on gender. Examples of this include:

- White blanc (masculine), blanche (feminine)

- Beautiful beau (masculine), belle (feminine)

- New nouveau (masculine), nouvelle (feminine)

- Soft fou (masculine), folle (feminine)

Usually, though, you simply add the masculine form of the adjective to make the feminine.

To use adjectives correctly in French, you have to know whether the noun you are describing is masculine or feminine. The article in front of the noun will tell you this. is used with masculine nouns and is used with feminine nouns. If the plural form of the noun is used the article will be and even though it is plural and you have to make the adjective plural, you still have to use the correct gender.

Look at these examples of how the adjectives are used:

• The green box?La boite verte. Box is considered a feminine noun and takes the feminine form of the adjective. The plural form, the green boxes, would be boites vertes?

• The grey truck as camion gris. The truck is a masculine word and takes the masculine form of the adjective. The plural form, the grey trucks, would be camion gris? The word already ends in, so you don't need to add another one.

When forming the plural of adjectives that end in you add the letter The adjective fou would then become foux in the plural form. The feminine form, folle, would take a to form the plural making it folles. Does the same rule apply to adjectives that end in such as in deal The plural form is deaux?

The placement of adjectives in sentences in the French language is also important. They usually follow the noun instead of coming in front of it. However, there are cases where the adjective does precede the noun and in some cases, this does require a change in how the word is spelled. If the noun being described begins with a vowel, then you have to change the spelling of the adjective. An example of this is in the use of the word To say a handsome boy, you can say un beau garcon, but to say, a handsome man, you have to say un bel home because the French word for man starts with h.

Where should you place French adjectives?

In English, you put adjectives before the noun they describe. So you'd say "a green bag", or "a blue house".

Most French adjectives are placed after the noun they describe. So you'd say "un sac vert" (lit: a bag green) or "une maison bleue" (lit: a house blue).

To remember that, imagine an Frenchman coming to you, and asking with a heavy (and charming) French accent "excuse me, where is the house blue?".

You could consider that French adjectives are placed after the noun they describe and would be correct in most situations, however, it's important to know there is an few exceptions.

Now come the bad boys or rather the BANGS boys:

• Beauty

• Age

• Number

• Goodness

• Size

Most adjectives expressing these (BANGS adjectives) are placed before the noun they describe.

• Une belle femme (a beautiful woman)

• Un vieil homme (a old man)

• Un gros sandwich (a big sandwich)

This is a useful rule to know but hardly an reliable one since there are many exceptions.

For example, some adjectives like "délicieux" (delicious) can come both before and after the noun they describe depending on the context

NOUN

All nouns in French have a gender, either masculine or feminine. For the most part, you must memorize the gender, but there are some endings of words that will help you decide which gender a noun is. Nouns ending in -age and -ment are usually masculine, as are nouns ending with a consonant. Nouns ending in -ure, -sion, -tion, -ence, -ance, -té, and -ette are usually feminine. Articles and adjectives must agree in number and gender with the nouns they modify. Articles have to be expressed even though they aren't always in English, and you may have to repeat the article in some cases. Demonstratives are like substantial definite articles.

French noun

French nouns can often function as other parts of speech such as verbs, auxiliary verbs, adverbs, and adjectives depending on their usage within the context of a sentence.

- être – being – noun, masculine

- dire – according to a – noun, masculine

- tout – all, everything, any – adj, indefinite adj.

- pouvior – power – noun, masculine

- bien – well, very good – adverb, noun

- devoir – duty – noun, masculine

- une chose – thing, matter – noun, feminine

- un petit – kid, child – noun

- merci – thanks, thank you – noun

- un peu – not much, not very, few – noun, adverb

- un homme – man – noun

- une femme – woman, wife – noun

- le temps – weather, time, times – noun

- la vie – life, lifetime, existence – noun

- le jour – day, daytime – noun

- un dieu – god – noun

- personne – anyone, anybody – indefinite pronoun, noun, feminine

- un père – father – noun

- une fille – daughter, girl, gal – noun

- le monde – world, people – noun

- un ami – friend, friendly – noun, adjective

- besoin – need, demand, necessity – noun, masculine

- accord – agreement, accord, harmony – noun, masculine

- monsieur – gentleman, Mr. – noun, masculine

- madame – madam, Mrs. – noun, feminine

- enfant – child, infant – noun

- grand – big, tall, large, great, big girl, big boy – adjective, noun

- mère – mother – noun, feminine

- maman – mummy, mama, mom – noun

- maison – house, home – noun, feminine

- nuit – night – noun, feminine

- peur – fear, fright – noun, feminine

- problème – problem – noun, masculine

- argent – silver, money – noun, masculine

- dernier – last, latest – adjective, noun, masculine

- tête – head, face – noun, feminine

- amour – love, love affair, cupid – noun, masculine

- nouveau – new, fresh – noun, adjective

- revoir – to see again, review – noun, masculine

- fait – event, fact – noun, masculine

- affaire – affair, business – noun, feminine

- frère – brother – noun, masculine

- histoire – history, story – noun, feminine

- jeune – young, youthful, young person – noun, masculine

- porte – gate, door – noun, feminine

- année – year – noun, feminine

- meilleur – better; the best one – adjective, noun

- place – room, square, seat – noun, feminine

- ville – town, city – noun, feminine

Plural Noun

Maybe you need to quickly get some notion of the French language, or maybe you are looking to start learning French as long commitment. Maybe it is for business, or maybe for pleasure. In any case, French lessons online are the best way to get you started, so today let's talk about French plural.

Forming the plural form of nouns is quite easy in French. As for any other language, there are rules you must follow, and exceptions you must know, but when you understand the concepts, it will be easy for you to use plural nouns. The basic rule to form the plural form of French nouns is to add an "s" to the word:

Singular - Plural

- Une carte (a card) - Des cartes (cards)

- Une chaise (a chair) - Des chaises (chairs)

- Une voiture (a car) - Des voitures (cars)

However, there are a couple of exceptions which are the words already ending in "s", "x" or "z" in their singular form. For those nouns, you do not need to change anything to form the plural version:

- Un nez (a nose) - Des nez (noses)

• Un bus (a bus) - Des bus (buses)

• Un prix (a price) - Des prix (prices)

And a few words will actually add an "x" in plural or completely change their spelling, but they are easy to remember:

• Un oiseau (a bird) - Des oiseaux (birds)

• Un oeil (an eye) - Des yeux (eyes)

As you can see, there are little tricks and notions to know. You must learn them and you will become fluent in French in no time. This can be sometime discouraging and boring but if you are serious and committed you will do great!

VERBS IN FRENCH

A very effective strategy for learning the complicated verb system in French is to focus on the most important verbs. Indeed, studies have shown that a tiny number of important verbs account for an large number of verbs used in the spoken language. The verbs presented here are the most common verbs that you will use in nearly every conversation. You should study them in detail in the biggest dictionary you can find and commit to memory the important tenses such as the Present, Compound Past, Imperfect, Future, and Present Subjunctive.

The first four verbs are what I call The Big Four. They are the key verbs in French because, in addition to having their own meanings and uses alone, they are helper verbs that are used in combination with other verbs to form idiomatic expressions. All of these verbs have irregular conjugations.

Irregular Conjugations Verb

1. ETRE (to be)

This is the granddaddy of French verbs. You will hear or use it in some form in nearly every second sentence in ordinary conversations. Etch the conjugations of this verb into your brain. One of the most common forms of this verb is in the phrase, c'est... (it is). Typical examples are c'est bon (it's good), c'est bien (it's fine), c'est beau (it's pretty), c'est la vie (such is life), c'est moi (it's me). This use is similar to what exists in English, but French has an unusual construction where the subject is used in combination with c'est. For example, in English, we say, "The law is the law." In French, we would say, La loi, c'est la loi. And "I'm the boss." is best translated by Le patron, c'est moi. One reason this verb is so important is that it is an auxiliary or helper verb. It is used to create the compound past of a small number of special verbs, as in:

- Je suis parti. (I left)

- Elle est venue. (She has come)

- Nous sommes descendus. (We went down)

2. AVOIR (to have)

The number two verb in French is a very common helper verb. In addition to having its own uses like j'ai de l'argent (I have some money), il n'a rien (he has nothing), AVOIR is used to form a series of idioms. such as:

avoir faim (to be hungry), avoir soif (to be thirsty), avoir froid (to be cold).

Probably, the most common use of this verb, is to form the compound past tense of all the verbs other than the small number that are conjugated with ETRE.

3. ALLER (to go)

The number three verb is a common helper verb when forming a future tense equivalent to the "I'm going to..." in English. Here are some examples:

- Je vais vous ouvrir la porte, madame. (I'll open the door for you, madam.)

- Nous allons partir demain. (We're going to leave tomorrow.)

4. FAIRE (to do / to make)

This particular verb has a rich set of meanings. It is used a lot when talking about the weather, as in, Il fait beau (The weather is nice). This is not to be confused with Il fait vieux (It/He looks old).

As a helping verb, faire is used an lot in combination with other verbs, as in:

- Il me fait rire. (He makes me laugh.)

- Faites voir. (Show me.)

- J'ai fait venir un livre. (I had a book sent to me)

5. POUVOIR (to be able, to can)

Uses include things like:

- Il peut vour recevoir maintenant. (He can see you now,)
- Je n'en peux plus. (I can't take it anymore.)
- There is an old spelling je puis that is used only in the question:
- Que puis-je faire pour vous? (What can I do for you?)

6. VOULOIR (to want, to desire)

Here are some examples:

- Je voudrais un verre de vin. (I would like a glass of wine.)
- Que voulez-vous que je fasse? (What do you want me to do?)

7. SAVOIR (to know)

- Elle ne sait pas nager. (She doesn't know how to swim.)
- Je ne le sais pas. (I don't know.)

8. DEVOIR (to have to, to be obliged to, to owe)

Here are some examples:

- Je dois partir. (I have to go.)
- Il me doit 10 dollars. (He owes me $10.)

9. VENIR (to come)

An interesting usage here is venir de + verb to mean "to have just".

- Je viens de manger. (I've just eaten.)
- Nous venons d'arriver. (We've just arrived.)

10. PRENDRE (to take)

Idiomatic usages include:

- Il a pris du poids. (He put on weight.)
- Elle se prend pour une vedette. (She thinks she is a star.)
- La police a pris les voleurs sur les faits. (The police caught the thieves red-handed.)

Common Irregular French Verbs

aller – to go

Je vais

Tu vas

Il/Elle va

Nous allons

Vous allez

Ils/Elles vont

Past Participle – allé

- ☐ avoir – to have
- ☐ J'ai
- ☐ Tu as
- ☐ Il/Elle a
- ☐ Nous avons
- ☐ Vous avez
- ☐ Ils/Elles ont

Past Participle – eu

- ☐ dire – to say, to tell

☐ Je dis

☐ Tu dis

☐ Il/Elle dit

☐ Nous disons

☐ Vous dites

☐ Ils/Elles disent

Past Participle – dit

- ☐ être – to be
- ☐ Je suis
- ☐ Tu es
- ☐ Il/Elle est
- ☐ Nous sommes
- ☐ Vous êtes
- ☐ Ils/Elles sont

Past Participle – été

- ☐ faire – to make, to do

- ☐ Je fais
- ☐ Tu fais
- ☐ Il/Elle fait
- ☐ Nous faisons
- ☐ Vous faites
- ☐ Ils/Elles – font

Past Participle – fait

- ☐ falloir – to be necessary
- ☐ Il faut

Past Participle – fallu

- ☐ pouvoir – to be able to do
- ☐ Je peux
- ☐ Tu peux
- ☐ Il/Elle peut
- ☐ Nous pouvons
- ☐ Vous pouvez
- ☐ Ils/Elles peuvent

Past Participle – pu

☐ savoir – to know, to know how to

- ☐ Je sais
- ☐ Tu sais
- ☐ Il/Elle sait
- ☐ Nous savons
- ☐ Vous savez
- ☐ Ils/Elles savent

Past Participle – su

- ☐ voir – to see
- ☐ Je vois
- ☐ Tu vois
- ☐ Il/Elle voit
- ☐ Nous voyons
- ☐ Vous voyez
- ☐ Ils/Elles voient

Past Participle – vu

- ☐ vouloir – to want to
- ☐ Je veux
- ☐ Tu veux
- ☐ Il/Elle veut
- ☐ Nous voulons
- ☐ Vous voulez
- ☐ Ils/Elles veulent

ADVERB IN FRENCH

If the word "adverb" scares you even in English, let's do a quick review. Simply put, adverbs describe verbs (action words) or adjectives (descriptive words). For example, take the sentence "Jack ran quietly through the very big library."The word "quietly" is an adverb because it describes how the verb "ran" was executed. (How did he run? Quietly.) Additionally, the word "very" is also an adverb because it describes the adjective "big." (How big? Very big.)

However, French handles adverbs a little differently than English. Don't stress, though, I've got all the tips to help you handle them smoothly.

French Adverbs That Modify Verbs

In English, adverb placement can be pretty complicated. For our purposes, however, let's just say that most of the time an adverb goes after the verb it modifies:

I read well.

But it can be quite flexible in many cases. Consider: "She quickly signed her name" and "She signed her name quickly."

Another tricky thing about English adverbs have to do with the placement of the adverb before or after an infinitive verb—but I'll let you Google "split infinitive" if you want in on that can of worms.

Is French adverb placement simpler, we hope?

Here's one general rule to rule (most of) them all: French adverbs go after the conjugated verb they modify.

Simple tenses

If the verb tense in question is a simple tense, the adverb goes right after the verb it modifies. That means that if a tense consists of only a conjugated main verb, the adverb goes after it. For example:

Je lis souvent.

(I read often.)

The adverb souvent (often) comes after the main, conjugated verb lis (read).

Compound tenses

However, if the verb tense being used is a compound tense, the adverb often goes after the support verb for short adverbs. That means that if a tense consists of the main verb and a support verb like être (to be), avoir (to have) or aller (to go), the adverb goes after the first conjugated verb. For example:

J'ai beaucoup dormi.

(I slept a lot.)

The adverb beaucoup comes after the conjugated support verb ai and before dormi.

There is some leeway, however. For longer adverbs, such as ones that end in -ment, the adverb can be placed after the participle. For example:

Je suis allé(e) rapidement à l'école.

(I went quickly to school.)

French Adverbs That Modify Adjectives

In English, adverbs usually come in front of the adjectives they modify:

I read very long books.

In French when an adverb modifies an adjective or another adverb, it's also placed in front of the word it modifies. Observe:

Tous les voyageurs que je connais sont vraiment sympas.

(All of the travelers I know are truly nice.)

The adverb vraiment comes before the adjective sympas, which it modifies.

Le film était trop bizarre pour moi.

(The film was too weird for me.)

The adverb trop comes before the adjective it modifies: bizarre.

You're Doing Well: Bon vs. Bien

Perhaps the most confusing of French adverb and adjective combinations are bon (good) and bien (well).

It turns out that adjectives and adverbs can be very friendly and close in meaning, but no two are closer than these two. They're so close, in fact, that they can be used as nouns as well, but in this section, we're just going to focus on their roles as adjectives.

To be clear:

Bon is an adjective meaning "good."

As such, bon modifies only nouns. For example, we could say "le bon garçon" to mean "the good boy." In this case, garçon is a noun, modified by the adjective bon. It would be incorrect to use bien in this situation.

The word bien is an adverb.

As you know, adverbs modify verbs or adjectives. In the case of bien, we could say "tu parles bien français" to mean "you speak French well." Parles is a verb, and the adverb bien modifies it. It would be incorrect to use bon in this situation. The same set-up goes for the adjective mauvais (bad) and the adverb mal (bad; poorly). While these words can be used as nouns in certain cases, mauvais is most often an adjective and modifies nouns.

Il a de mauvais résultats.

(He has bad results.)

Mal is most often an adverb and modifies a verb.

J'ai mal mangé.

(I didn't eat well.)

When French Adjectives Transform into Adverbs

Remember how I said adjectives and adverbs were close?

Well, like English, French allows adjectives to become adverbs by adding a suffix. In English, that suffix is "–ly." For example, we can take the adjective "obvious" and turn it into the adverb "obviously" by adding the suffix "-ly."

The same is true for French. By adding the suffix -ment, French speakers can transform adjectives into adverbs. For example:

confortable (comfortable) → confortablement (comfortably)

malheureuse (unfortunate) → malheureusement (unfortunately)

Not so fast, though. French has a few rules for transforming adjectives into adverbs:

1. If the adjective finishes with a vowel, simply add the suffix -ment.

facile (easy) → facilement (easily)

2. If the adjective ends in a consonant, you must add the suffix -ment to the feminine form of the adjective. For example:

réel (real) → réelle (real-feminine form) → réellement (really)

3. If the adjective finishes with -ent or -ant, you simply remove those letters and instead add -emment or -amment respectively. Like so:

évident (evident) → évidemment (evidently)

brillant (brilliant) → brillamment (brilliantly)

Keep in mind, however, that there are a few exceptions.

We already spoke about how the adverb form of the adjective bon is bien, and other irregular adverbs include gentiment (nicely) from the adjective gentil (nice) and brièvement (briefly) from the adjective bref (brief).

Common French Adverbs

- Assez (quite, fairly)
- Il est assez bon.
- (He is quite good.)
- Toujours (always)
- Vous regardez toujours ces émissions.
- (You always watch these television shows.)
- Parfois (sometimes)
- Je vais parfois à la bibliothèque.
- (I sometimes go to the library.)
- Rarement (rarely)
- Nous sortons rarement.
- (We rarely go out.)
- Maintenant (now)
- Elle mange maintenant.
- (She is eating now.)
- Tard (late, later)
- Tu arrives tard.
- (You're arriving late.)
- Très (very)
- Le repas est très bon.
- (The meal is very good.)
- Trop (too much)
- Ils parlent trop.
- (They speak too much.)
- Rapidement (quickly)
- Elles lisent rapidement.
- (They read quickly.)
- Lentement (slowly)
- Répétez lentement, s'il vous plaît.

CHAPTER TWO:
GREETINGS IN FRENCH

Kinds Of French Greetings!

If you are planning to travel to France, Canada, Quebec, or any of the numerous French speaking countries, the first thing you need to do is to learn how to present yourself.Don't worry, it is extremely easy, and here I will show you the different kinds of greetings, and explain why you should use this one instead of that. We assume that you are the English Native (John) and that you are talking with a French native (Marc).

Note: Marc is a common French name. Be careful, Mark doesn't take a K at the end (like the name Mark).

Ok, ready? Let's start.

Formal French Greetings (Adults)

John: Bonjour! = Hello!

Marc: Bonjour!

John: Comment allez-vous? = How are you doing? Or How are you?

Marc: Je vais bien, Merci. I'm fine thanks.

Explanation: you can use this form of French Greetings in a business context without any problem. You can also use it in an interview.

However, this is not modern French, and as we will see, it is not for the youngers. This kind of Greetings is used by adults only. As a teen, I've never said bonjour to one of my friends...

2) French Greetings (Teenagers)

John: Salut, ca va? = Hi, How are you doing?

Marc: Ca va, et toi? = Fine, what about you?

John: Tu fais quoi là? = What are you doing right now?

Marc: Je vais an l' école = I'm going to school

In this case, two teenagers are talking. Note that they are not using the famous bonjour!

3) French Greetings (slang)

John: Ca se passe Marc? = Everything is OK Marc?

Marc: Tranquille = Smooth, no problems.

John: Quoi de neuf? = What's new?

Marc: Rien que du vieux! = Only old news!

This form of Greetings is Slang. You do not want to use it with adults or at work... Teenagers use to speak like this. They use the modern French language which tends to vary from one department to another.You know have three different ways to say Hi. According to the situation, use the appropriate one. Be aware that the French language is really rich, and that what you are learning right now can be an old French which is not used any more!

Advice for everybody who wants to learn modern French: do your homeworks! You need to be sure that your teachers are real French speakers who actually lived in France! Not one year or two, but decades...

Useful French Greetings phrase

Say Hello

1. Bonjour! – Hello! (Also, Good Morning!)

This is your run of the mill, basic French greeting, and it works in any setting, formal and informal alike. It's probably the first word that most French language beginners learn, and for good reason! It's only common courtesy to utter a little bonjour to the baker as you walk into the corner boulangerie or to the waiter before you order a coffee on the terrasse of a Parisian café. Not using this greeting is deemed utterly impolite by many and may merit a disdainful glance.

Once the sun sets, you'll want to replace this little pleasantry with bonsoir! (Good evening!) All in all, using either bonjour or bonsoir is your best bet for first greeting someone in either a formal or informal setting.

2. Salut! – Hi!

This is a great greeting to use with anyone you see rather often or someone you know rather well, i.e. a colleague with similar standing as you or a good friend. It is an informal greeting and should be used as such since it is not exactly an expression you'll want to whip out at to begin a business meeting.

Note that the "t" on the end of the word is silent, thus following the general rule in French that if a final consonant is not followed by an "e" or another vowel, it is not pronounced.

3. Coucou! – Hey there!

This is an extremely informal way of greeting someone, so reserve this one for close friends and family, otherwise, you might get a few quizzical stares. As an added tidbit, the verb phrase faire coucou (à quelqu'un) means to wave at or say hey (to someone), and is also a form of informal language.

Adding on to that, the verb phrase jouer à coucou means to play peekabooas a mother does with her baby. Thus, you can see the rather playful and familiar tone behind this word.

4. Quoi de neuf? – What's up?

While remaining informal, this is a slightly more involved greeting, in that you're likely to glean more from the person you are speaking with than you would with the traditional bonjour. This literally means "what's new?" and is an excellent greeting to use with a friend you haven't spoken with in a while, with the intent of starting a conversation.

5. Allô? – Hello?

While a cognate of English, this is not used in the same capacity as bonjour, in that you cannot use it to greet people on the street. This greeting is used solely on the phone to determine whether or not someone is on the line. It can also be used ironically to get the attention of someone that hasn't heard you, the point is that it's as though the person wasn't there. You probably won't hear it used in any other situations.

Useful French Phrases

to Say Goodbye

1. Au revoir! – Goodbye!

This expression, like bonjour, is another go-to standard salutation, usable in virtually any situation: as you leave the hair salon, as you leave the bus, as you take leave from an acquaintance, etc. Like bonjour or bonsoir, it is considered rude to not use this particular expression in public, as well as over the phone, just before hanging up.Yet a lot of French people tend to slur these two words together, so it can sometimes just sound like "ohrvwar."

2. Salut! – Bye-bye!

That's right, double whammy! Salut can be used to say both hi and bye. As is the case with greeting someone, bidding someone farewell with this expression is also quite informal. Overall, a very useful little word to know.

3. Je suis désolé(e), mais je dois y aller – I'm sorry, but I have to go

This phrase doesn't have a particular spot on either end of the formal/informal scale. The main idea with this expression is its sense of urgency, and it is the je dois y aller which relays this message. The pronoun y must be used before the verb aller if no particular location is mentioned.

If you want to be more explicit and state exactly where you are going, for example, I have to go to school, then the sentence would look like this: Je dois aller à l'école.

Another example would be I have to go to the museum: Je dois aller au musée. The Je suis désolé(e) simply shows that you are sorry for leaving, literally meaning I am sorry. Note that when the speaker is feminine, an extra "e" is needed at the end. This doesn't change the pronunciation of the word, it is merely a grammatical aspect of the language which is only evident on paper.

4. À plus tard! (À plus!) – (See you) later!

This is a useful expression for when you know you will see someone again, such as a friend or classmate, but you're not quite sure when that will be. It is not particularly formal or informal, granted you will only use this expression when you know someone well enough to see them on at least a semi-regular basis. Note that pronunciation differs depending on which expression you decide to go with. If you go with the shorter version, the "s" on the end of plus is indeed pronounced. Yep, it's an exception to the general rule of pronunciation!

5. À tout à l'heure! – See you soon, See you in a while!

This is the perfect expression to use for if you are parting with friends that you are certain to see again later in the day.

Take it up a notch: Désolé(e), mais je dois filer! – Sorry, but I gotta run!

This is a little phrase you can use in informal settings, for example when you have to leave a group of friends rather abruptly. The désolé(e) (sorry) renders this phrase polite so that you don't have to worry about offending anyone.

Dos and Don'ts for French Greetings

The proper etiquette for greeting people in France relies on a few factors. While it's expected and considered polite to greet everyone, from colleagues to shopkeepers, the way you greet each person depends on your relationship with them and the social setting. For example...

Les bises (kisses) is a typical greeting when meeting friends in France.

Depending on the region of France, la bise can include one, two, or even three little kisses on the cheek. If in doubt, let the other person initiate and move to one side of your face or the other. The kisses generally begin on the right side of the face.

 handshake is a greeting that is reserved for formal or business settings.

When entering a meeting for work, it's normal for colleagues to offer a firm handshake. It's also common for men to greet with a handshake rather than with une bise.

A hug, contrary to American greetings, is reserved for close family members or significant others only.

FAREWELLS IN FRENCH

Say goodbye (or otherwise end a conversation) in French:

Au revoir. (Oh reh-vwah) This is the most common ways of saying goodbye in French, and it's acceptable for the vast majority of situations, formal and informal. It literally means "until we each see each other again."

Bonne journée / Bonne soirée. (Bun zhoor nay / Bun swah ray) These phrases mean: "Have a good day/ Have a good evening," respectively, and they are typical ways of ending a conversation. You are acceptable in formal and informal settings. For example, it's common to use it when ending a conversation with a client, or leaving a store or restaurant.

À tout à l'heure. (Ah too tah leuhr). This means "see you later." This phrase is used if you will see the person later in the day. It's acceptable in both formal and informal situations.

À plus tard (Ah plue tahr). This phrase also means "see you later" but is only used in more informal circumstances. You may also hear it said as "à plus" (ah plue-ss), which is just an abbreviation. In informal emails, you may see it written as A+.

À bientôt (Ah bee yen toe). This is general ways of saying "see you soon." You'd use it formally or casually when you know you'll be seeing the person soon. If you're seeing the person within a matter of hours, you could say À très bientôt. (See you very soon).

À tout de suite (Ah too deh sweet). Here's yet another way of saying "see you very soon." The key distinction is that you'd only say it when you're seeing the person immediately following your conversation. For example, if you were having a conversation with a friend about where to meet, and you were planning to meet right afterwards, you could end the conversation with "à tout de suite."

À la prochaine (Ah la prosh-enne). This phrase means "until next time" or "see you next time." Unsurprisingly, it's used when you're unsure of when you're going to see the other person again.

À demain (A deh-mahn). This phrase means "until tomorrow" or "see you tomorrow." Naturally, it's for use when you're certain of seeing the person you're speaking to tomorrow.

Salut (Sah-lou). This is a very casual way of saying goodbye (or rather, 'bye!) in French. Note that it also means "hi!"

Adieu (Ah d'yew) Use this rather somber goodbye word only when you know you will never see the person again. Literally, it means "until God," which gives you a strong clue as to the sense of finality it imparts.

Hospitality

It was a soft summer night. Still light at 8:30. And comfortably warm after the day's searing heat. Yer hero (that's me, folks) was in his third hour of surfing this tiny perfect French village. It was the ole "good news - bad news" deal. The good news - everyone I met was more than overjoyed, delighted, and, yes, salivating at the prospect of having the exotic stranger from the far awaylands(thats me, again, folks) dazzle them with his guitar artistry in exchange for a bed n' grub. The bad news - all of the everyones were otherwise committed.

No Room at the Inn

The village Mayoress DID have guests. So, would have been perfect - except she'd already booked a cellist. Oh well! Jean-Marc, the baker had a housefull. Lucian, the IT guy("information technology" - the French way of saying - "computer nerd") had, not only a young baby but also a 6 am a wake-up call. (Read - no sleep for anyone in that house!) Logically, this village was a loser. Lotsagood vibes, but no possibility.Logically, most folks would have shuffled on down da road.

Quitters never Win

But, as my regular readers know, da BG's battery does not run on logic. It's fired by heart. By the vibe of the people and the place.My engines fuel is FAITH. Unquestioned, unshakeable faith in the goodness of human nature. All this, unconsciously confirming that the magic combo of interest and possibility DID, indeed exist here. Simply a matter 'o keepin' on, keepin' on.

Faith rewarded

Earlier in my noble quest, I was advised by three sisters(not really sisters, actually, but, more on that later)to knock on a certain door down the street from them. This I did. Several times over the course of three hours. To no avail. However, as I made yet another pass through perfect village-land, I did spy a booty-ful woman (and aren't they the best kind?) walking in my direction on the opposite side of the street. Naturally, I was instinctively compelled to point my steed in her direction. And, after her very friendly, smiling "bonjour" was further compelled to explain my gig.Jana, then suggested it might be possible at her house. And beckoned me to follow. You know what's coming next, dear reader, do you not? Indeed. Jana's house was the one I was pointed to by the 3 (faux) sisters.

A Load off my Brains

After installing me on her sun dappled patio with a tall, cool one,(non-alcoholic) Jana warned soberly: "It's alright with me, but, of course, my Husband could say no." You're ahead of me again, are'nt you? Happily for me (and this non-ribald tale) Roland, the Husband not only didn't say no but enthusiastically peppered me with questions, while Jana made up my room. (Actually, a suite!)

The Thick Plotens

After a long, refreshing shower, I returned to the patio to find the three (faux), sisters. Who were, in fact, Grandma, Daughter, and (teen-age) Daughter. They had each, thoughtfully, arrived with a bottle. To compliment the massive two litres one Roland had produced. Muchies festooned the table. Twilight crept on. The night stayed warm. The welcome was warmer. And so, a very memorable evening of wine,women(two men) and song. (Not to mention some great grub!)

Morning way

Next, am, after a deep and peaceful sleep, I awoke to freshly baked goodies and strong Italian coffee on the patio. Again caressed by the sun and a soft breeze.

After the farewell photos, exchanging emails, etc. your hero saddled up, and rode happily into the daybreak. But wait - There's More! As I passed the house of the three(not really) sisters, poised to give them a hearty goodbye wave, they were on the front lawn wavin' me in.

My Arm Twisted Again

Now, I ask you, dear reader, after the wonderful night we'all had passed together, it would have been the height of bad manners NOT to accept their luncheon invitation - would it not?

But wait - (again) - This is NOT the punchline. The punchline is - This was two years ago. And since then, at every possible card/email sending opportunity - Christmas, New year's, Easter, I get a message along the lines of "we never forget the wonderful time we spent together, and hope all is well with you." Now that, folks, is HOSPITALITY! N'est ce pas?

COURTESY IN FRENCH

When it comes to good manners both the English and Frenchman in me are equally convinced that in a civilized society generally-agreed codes of respect and consideration towards others - especially when strangers or barely known - are vital in reducing the risk of conflict or offence in the requests, agreements, refusals, apologies, greetings and partings which are so much a part of our everyday lives. Both are also not without knowing that polite behaviour consists in maintaining a fine balance between showing you think well of others, and not giving others the impression you think too well of yourself.My Frenchman is inclined to think it is those Puritan values of modest self-effacement and informal simplicity which have caused you English to incline less towards showing others (in appearance at least) you think well of yourselves, and more towards demonstrating to others that you think well of them. For he will never cease to be surprised by the monotonous frequency with which you use those words 'please' and 'thank you' and, above all, by the humble, apologetic type of civility you generally adopt towards those who are paid to serve you directly. I mean, who else but you English could thank the dustbin man for being considerate enough to empty your wheelie bin, the postman for going so far out of his way to pop your mail through the letterbox, and the bus driver for showing such exquisite courtesy in actually bringing his vehicle to a halt at your stop? And I will never understand why, in a café, you say, 'Could I possibly have a Cappuccino and a Brownie please?' or, 'I'm awfully sorry to bother you but could I have the bill, please?' in such a deferential tone of voice, when it's the waitress's job to do exactly this. Or, when the home help arrives in the morning, instead of giving her polite but firm instructions on what you require to be done, you give the house a good clean beforehand, and then apologize for the mess it's in when she finally turns up!

What's more, I'd be willing to bet my bottom euro that there isn't another country on our planet where direct rectification, disagreement or contradiction is perceived as being tantamount to a declaration of war. I mean, it can only be you English who, when you find yourselves in the embarrassing position of having to correct a mistake, will go to such extraordinarily apologetic lengths to point out that what you're about to say should in no way be considered a criticism, but stems merely from the wish to explain. Though I'd be the first to admit that the rules of politeness oblige us - often hypocritically - to conceal our true feelings and opinions so as to minimize the risk of conflict with others, you take this to ridiculous extremes. I really don't know any other people who, instead of declaring, 'No, I disagree with you entirely!' will go to such extraordinary lengths to reply, 'Well, you certainly might have a point but, on the other hand, don't you think that... ?' when they are intimately convinced you're talking unmitigated rubbish. Now let's be honest. How can you possibly trust someone who systematically professes to agree with everything you say?

Moreover, I might even go so far as to say that your English reluctance to indulge in what could be remotely construed as straight-to-the-point discord would appear to be even stronger than your puritanically-inspired distrust of outward show. Take that occasion when, after landing in England early one Friday evening, I caught a train from the airport station. The next stop was a large town where the train filled up with people going home from work. Barely had I settled down to have a quiet read when my attention was drawn to a pin-stripe-suited gentleman sitting at the far end of the carriage who had just begun talking loudly into his cell phone - so loudly, in fact, that it would have taken someone with the hearing capacities of a stone to have escaped what he was saying.

The gentleman, we were quickly made to understand, occupied some high managerial position in an insurance company, and his discussions were focused on the financial consequences of a fire which, apparently, had ravaged the premises of a large local company the previous day. But just as one interminable conversation ended, someone else was contacted, and more or less the same sort of discussion began again. I remember thinking it strange that he should be disclosed to any Tom, Dick or Harry what normally would have called for quiet discretion when the truth of the matter suddenly dawned. The financial discussions were secondary. The main aim of all this was to impress upon the captive audience of a commuter train's second class carriage that they had been granted the privilege of sharing a moment in the professional life of a man who had nothing to envy a Dallas soap opera oil baron. In short, he was just showing off.

Now, had we been in France it would certainly have been politely but firmly brought to his notice at an early stage that this one-man ego show was becoming intrusive. It might even have been pointed out that, given their confidential nature, his discussions might be more appropriately confined to the privacy of his office. But here in England, everybody bore up with the fortitude of a Stoic philosopher resigning himself to unavoidable necessity: not a word of complaint was to be heard, and we were subjected to an hour or more of uninterrupted talk (the businessman's telephonic partners were strangely mute). However, our man, I noted, repeatedly made the same, rather amusing grammatical errors: he was, for example, particularly fond of beginning his sentences with 'But, the point being is that. I mustn't have been the only person to have noticed this, for a young woman sitting nearby could control herself no longer and burst out into a fit of uncontrolled laughter - so contagious, in fact, that it quickly spread to most of the carriage's occupants. It took only a couple of minutes for our businessman to realize that in the eyes of his audience his performance was being perceived more and more like that of a clown: for he promptly lowered his voice to an inaudible whisper, and a few seconds later sheepishly switched off his mobile before seeking shameful refuge behind the outstretched pages of his Financial Times.

Courtesy Phase

Thank you,   Merci

No thank you. Non Merci

You are welcome De rien

Please   S'il vous plait

Excuse me Excusez moi

I am sorry. Je suis desole

Forgive me. Pardonnez-moi

You are very nice. Vous etes tres gentil

Thank you for your help Merci de votre aide

Misunderstanding in french.

Yep, that's right. I said it out loud.

 Lived in Paris and have French friends, and once I started to understand the culture I started to understand the French. What we perceive as rude behaviour in cafes and restaurants, shops, etc, is simply this - the French are a fiercely proud race.

And aren't we all? In our own countries, don't we have pride too?

So - what's the difference? How can we overcome this misconception?

There. I've said it. The simplest thing in the world. Learn a few words and phrases and make a tiny effort, and you'll be amazed at the response.

Start off with Hello, Goodbye, Thank you, You're welcome, See you soon ... get the idea?

Bonjour! Au revoir. Merci De rien! A bientot!

Bonjour, je m'appelle ...

Hello, my name is.

Monkey see monkey do

Watching how the French behave when they enter a store - any store - and when they leave. They say BONJOUR to the men and women already in the store, which shows politesse, is appreciated by all and is customary.Customary, you say? Yes! When in another country, follow some basic customs and show respect, and you'll receive the same in return.

The French people also say goodbye to everyone as they leave a store. It's expected, and if you follow suit, even stumbling over what to say, at least you will have made an effort. Trust me - it will be noticed and appreciated.

If I YELL, will you understand English???

Oh boy - this is a biggie. In all my years of travelling, I'm constantly amazed when I see foreigners who speak loud enough to be yelling, trying to get a local person to UNDERSTAND what they're saying.

HELLOOOOOO!!! Yelling doesn't mean you're a language translator.

I know that's a shock, but it's true.

I don't know where or how or why this ever started, but it continues worldwide.

Don't yell in English to a foreigner who doesn't seem to understand what you're saying. Pull out your phrase book instead and have a go at speaking French.

You might be pleasantly surprised when the other person tries to communicate more willingly.

Thank you! THANK YOU! Merci! Merci beaucoup!

Saying PLEASE and THANK YOU is important in all languages, no matter where you are. It's no different in France.

"Please ..." = "S'il vous plait ..." [pronounce as Seel voo play]

"Thank you." = "Merci." [pronounce as Mare-see]

"Thank you very much!" = "Merci beaucoup!"

Even if this is ALL you say, say it a LOT.

Smiling, scowling or indifferent?

I'm a happy person - I talk to strangers EVERYwhere, I do, because I like to. Not everyone is the same, and just because you're bubbling with enthusiasm when you're in Paris, don't expect everyone else to be as happy or gushy as you.In my experience, French people are more reserved than in the USA or Australiia and do not necessarily want to smile at beaming strangers.

Use your judgement here ... if you learn a few words of French and can say it's a beautiful day, you'll have more chance of getting a smile or a response than just beaming a great big smile.Please don't be offended if people do not always smile back at you - think about your own town or city or village ... not everyone's exactly the same, with the same personality, are they? If you treat people with respect and courtesy, you'll receive it in return.

THE COLOUR = LA COULEUR

The colours = Les couleurs

English   French

Red Le Rouge

Yellow.   Le Jaune

Blue   Le Bleu (m), bleue (f)

Black Le Noir (m), noire (f)

White   Le Blanc (m), Blanche (f)

Green Le Vert (m), Verte (f)

Orange   L'Orange

Grey Le Gris (m), grise (f)

Pink Le Rose

Silve L' Argent (m)

Gold L' Or (m)

Grey (Eng) / gray (USA) Le Gris (m), Grise (f)

Brown   Le Marron

Purple   Le Pourpre

Violet   Le Violet (m), Violette (f

French Costumes Colour

Traditionally, the French Maid costume was black and white but as the costume has grown in popularity, so has the color choices. There are many variations as far as exposure, style, and color so it is a sexy costume that can accommodate everyone.

1. Black and White - This is how it all started. The maid in her black dress and white apron. When people refer to this costume, this is the color choice that visually pops in their mind. This color scheme of the costume is known worldwide.

2. Red and Black - Room service anyone? A great variation to the traditional costume is the maid/room service costume. She looks a bit like bell hop who will be more than happy to escort you to your room, and then she'll clean it for you too.

3. Pink - All maids look great in pink. The pink French Maid is sexy yet innocent all rolled into one. Pink is a youthful color that represents a bit of innocence. Pairing this color up with the French Maid costume is sure to turn a few heads.

4. White - the color of everything that is pure. White French Maid costumes take a sweet, pure color and make it sassy. This is usually paired up with baby blue or you could choose to put a different color petticoat under the skirt for a truly original look.

5. Red and White - The checkered little red and white costume is the perfect "home-maker" maid. She is going to clean your entire house from top to bottom and bake you an apple pie while she's doing it.

Whatever color you choose for your sexy French Maid costume, make it work for you. If you want traditional, opt for the black and white. If you are a daring kind of gal and really want to turn some heads and have some fun, check out the different color options available.

NUMERALS AND NUMBERS IN FRENCH

French number

Un, deux, trois, c'est parti (one, two, three, here we go)!

So... you want to learn how to count in French like a pro?

Well, look no further mes amis, because this book will teach you how to do it—en un tour de main (in a flash)!

The key to learning how to count in French from 100 to 1000 is to learn the first hundred numbers, from 1 to 100; all you have to do after that is just put on the front cent (one hundred), or deux cent (two hundred), or trois cent (three hundred), or quatre cent (four hundred), or cinq cents (five hundred), etc.

Plutôt facile, non? (rather easy, no?)

Prenons quelques exemples (let us take a few examples), to make it even clearer:

7 = Sept, 700 = Sept cent, 707 = Sept cent sept

307 = Trois cent sept

801 = Huit cent un

18 = Dix-huit, 100 = cent, 118 = Cent dix-huit

918 = Neuf cent dix-huit

* D'abord (first), the first 100 numbers in French:

0 Zéro	4 Quatre	8 Huit
1 Un	5 Cinq	9 Neuf
2 Deux	6 Six	10 Dix
3 Trois	7 Sept	11 Onze

12 Douze

13 Treize

14 Quatorze

15 Quinze

16 Seize

17 Dix-sept

18 Dix-huit

19 Dix-neuf

20 Vingt

21 Vingt et un

22 Vingt-deux

23 Vingt-trois

24 Vingt-quatre

25 Vingt-cinq

26 Vingt-six

27 Vingt-sept

28 Vingt-huit

29 Vingt-neuf

30 Trente

31 Trente et un

32 Trente-deux

33 Trente-trois

34 Trente-quatre

35 Trente-cinq

36 Trente-six

37 Trente-sept

38 Trente-huit

39 Trente-neuf

40 Quarante

41 Quarante et un

42 Quarante-deux

43 Quarante-trois

44 Quarante-quatre

45 Quarante-cinq

46 Quarante-six

47 Quarante-sept

48 Quarante-huit

49 Quarante-neuf

50 Cinquante

51 Cinquante et un

52 Cinquante-deux

53 Cinquante-trois

54 Cinquante-quatre

55 Cinquante-cinq

56 Cinquante-six

57 Cinquante-sept

58 Cinquante-huit

59 Cinquante-neuf

60 Soixante

61 Soixante et un

62 Soixante-deux

63 Soixante-trois

64 Soixante-quatre

65 Soixante-cinq

66 Soixante-six

67 Soixante-sept

68 Soixante-huit

69 Soixante-neuf

70 Soixante-dix

71 Soixante et onze

72 Soixante-douze

73 Soixante-treize

74 Soixante-quatorze

75 Soixante-quinze

76 Soixante-seize

77 Soixante-dix-sept

78 Soixante-dix-huit

79 Soixante dix-neuf

80 Quatre-vingts (Literally "Four twenties"!)

81 Quatre-vingt-un

82 Quatre-vingt-deux

83 Quatre-vingt-trois

84 Quatre-vingt-quatre

85 Quatre-vingt-cinq

86 Quatre-vingt-six

87 Quatre-vingt-sept

88 Quatre-vingt-huit

89 Quatre-vingt-neuf

90 Quatre-vingt-dix

91 Quatre-vingt-onze

92 Quatre-vingt-douze

93 Quatre-vingt-treize

94 Quatre-vingt-quatorze

95 Quatre-vingt-quinze

96 Quatre-vingt-seize

97 Quatre-vingt-dix-sept

98 Quatre-vingt-dix-huit

99 Quatre-vingt dix-neuf

100 Cent

101 Cent un

102 Cent deux

103 Cent trois .etc.

TIME AND DATE

Say Dates and Times in French

Days of the week and months

The days of the week (les jours de la semaine) aren't capitalized in French.

i. lundi (luhn-DEE) (Monday)

ii. mardi (mahr-DEE) (Tuesday)

iii. mercredi (mehr-kruh-DEE) (Wednesday)

iv. jeudi (juh-DEE) (Thursday)

v. vendredi (vahn-druh-DEE) (Friday)

vi. samedi (sahm-DEE) (Saturday)

vii. dimanche (dee-MAHNSH) (Sunday)

Like the days of the week, the months of the year (les mois de l'année) aren't capitalized in French.

i. janvier (zhahng-VYAY) (January)

ii. février (fay-VRYAY) (February)

iii. mars (mahrs) (March)

iv. avril (ah-VREEL) (April)

v. mai (meh) (May)

vi. juin (zhwang) (June)

vii. juillet (zhwee-YAY) (July)

viii. août (oot) (August)

ix. septembre (set-TAHMBR) (September)

x. octobre (ock-TOHBR) (October)

xi. novembre (noh-VAHMBR) (November)

xii. décembre (day-SAHMBR) (December)

TELLING TIME

The time of day can be described in general terms or specific times. You can use the following words to describe the general time of day.

• le matin (morning)

• l'après-midi (afternoon)

• le soir (evening)

• la nuit (night)

• le jour (day)

• midi (noon)

• minuit (midnight)

• aujourd'hui (today)

• hier (yesterday)

• demain (tomorrow)

When you want to know a specific time of day, you can ask Quelle heure est-il? (What time is it?). Although we usually leave off the 'o'clock' when we say a specific time, you must always include the heure (hour/time) when expressing a specific time in French. The only real exception to this is midi (noon) or minuit (midnight).When expressing time between the hours, use the following terms to break things down.

• l'heure (hour/time/clock/watch)

• minute (minute)

• seconde (second)

• et demie (half past)

• et quart (quarter past)

• moins le quart (quarter till)

• moins dix (10 till [literally: minus 10 minutes])

The French generally express time using a 24-hour clock. So, 4 p.m. would be seized heures (16 hours). However, you can use du matin (in the morning) and du soir (in the evening) if you want to express time using the standard 12-hour clock.

You can use the following phrases as a guide when talking about time in French.

• Avez-vous une minute? (Do you have a minute?)

• Avez-vous l'heure? (Do you have the time?)

• Quelle heure est-il? (What time is it?)

• Il est tard. (It's late.

• Il est tôt. (It's early.

• Il est huit heures du matin. (It's 8 in the morning.)

• Il est midi. (It's noon.)

• Il est cinq heures de l'après-midi. (It's 5 in the afternoon.)

• Il est sept heures du soir. (It's 7 in the evening.)

• Il est sept heures et quart. (It's a quarter past 7.)

• Il est sept heures et demie. (It's 7:30.)

• Il est huit heures moins le quart. (It's a quarter to 8.)

CHAPTER THREE:
FAMILY AND FRIENDS IN FRENCH

FAMILY AND FRIEND

Family is an important concept for many of us, no matter where we live or what language we speak. It's something that bonds us together. Now that you're learning French, it is likely that you may want to talk about your family members in your new language. This lesson will give you the vocabulary to do just that.

The word for family in French is une famille, (oon fah-mee).

It may help to imagine a French family to try out some new French vocabulary. While we look at the family imagined here, think of your own and see if any of the new words might apply.

Family tree and how to say family in French?

In French the word 'family' we translate as 'famille', it' consists of close relatives, such as your father, sister, uncle, cousin, etc.

Start with Sandrine. She lives in Bordeaux, in southwest France, with her immediate family.

She has two parents. The word for parents in French is very similar to our own: des parents, (day par-ahn).

She has a mother, une mère, (oon mehr), and a father, un père, (uhn pehr). In French, you might also hear the familiar forms of these words, Maman, (Mah-mahn), and Papa, (Pah-pah).

Her family has four children in it. The word in French for children is des enfants, (dayz ahn-fahn).

Sandrine has two sisters. The word for sister is une sœur, (oon sör). She has one brother, un frère, (uhn frehr). He is the baby, le bébé, (luh bay-bay).

When we say that Sandrine has two sisters and one brother, it also tells us that her parents have three daughters and one son. The word for daughter is une fille, (oon fee), and the word for son is un fils, (uhn fees).

What about your family tree? How is it like Sandrine's? How is it different?

Let's practice a tiny bit with this vocabulary, so you can see how you might apply it to yourself.

To say, 'I have children,' you would say, J'ai des enfants.

If you'd like to say, 'I have a son and a daughter. I also have a sister and a brother,' you might say, 'J'ai un fils et une fille. J'ai aussi (also) une sœur et un frère.'

Notice the expression J'ai, (jay). It means 'I have'.

If you like to make it negative (to say you don't have any), you'll change it to je n'ai pas de, (juh nay pah duh) as in, Je n'ai pas de filles. 'I don't have any daughters'.

Extended Family

Let's add some members to Sandrine's family. Sandrine's extended family lives further east, in the Burgundy region.

Sandrine, like many of us, has grandparents. She's their granddaughter.

Let's see that same idea in French: see if you can find the word for grandparents in the first sentence!

If you guessed that des grand-parents, (day grah-pah-rahn), was the French word for grandparents, you were right! She has a grandmother, une grand-mère, (oon grahn-mehr), and a grandfather, un grand-père, (uhn grahn-pehr). The word for granddaughter, as you can see it in the sentence above, is une petite-fille. For grandson, it's un petit-fils. And for grandchildren, it's des petits-enfants, (day puh-teez ahn-fahn).

Sandrine also has aunts, uncles, and cousins. Her favorite aunt is une tante, (oon tahnt), or Tata, in the familiar form, as we might say Auntie. Her closest uncle is un oncle, (uhn ohn-cl), or Tonton, in the most familiar form. A male cousin is un cousin, (uhn coo-zan), and a female cousin is une cousine, (oon coo-zeen).

Sandrine doesn't have any nieces and nephews yet, but you might! The word for niece is une nièce, (oon nee-ess). The word for nephew is un neveu, (uhn nev-ö).

English French

parents les parents

mother la maman /la mère

father le papa/le père

children les enfants

son le fils

daughter la fille

nephew le neveu

niece la nièce

brother le frère

sister la soeur

English French

aunt la tante

uncle l'oncle

godfather le parrain

godmother la marraine

grandparents les grands-parents

grandmother la grand-mère

grandfather le grand-père

grandson le petit-fils

grand-daughter la petite-fille

Sandrine a des grand-parents. Sandrine est leur petite-fille.

In-law in French -Members of Family

Your family in-law is formed on the one hand by the members of your spouse's family. But it can also be formed by the family members of a remarriage, for example after a divorce. Here is a detailed list of vocabulary to describe your family in-laws:

English	French
family-in-law conjoint)	La belle-famille (du côté du
stepparents	Les beaux-parents (d'un remariage)
parents-in-law conjoint)	Les beaux-parents (du côté du
stepfather	Le beau-père (d'un remariage)
stepmother	La belle-mère (d'un remariage)
mother in law	La belle-mère (du côté du conjoint)
stepdaughter	La belle-fille (d'un remariage)
daughter-in-law	La belle-fille (du côté du conjoint)
stepson	Le beau-fils (d'un remariage)
son-in-law	Le gendre (du côté du conjoint)
sister-in-law	La belle-sœur (du côté du conjoint)
sister-in-law	La belle-sœur (d'un remariage)
brother-in-law	Le beau-frère (du côté du conjoint)
brother-in-law	Le beau-frère (d'un remariage)

FRIENDS

How do you say "friends" in French

Ami (m), amie (f) - the most commonly found, usually denoting a true and sincere friendship.

Copain (m), copine (f) - applies to a warm relation with someone, yet not intimate enough to be considered as meaningful as a deep friendship. Often used for a person one recently met and hangs out with a lot.

Pote (informal) - is mostly used among youngsters. Usually describes a casual but regular encounter, often somebody with whom one shares common activity or leisure.

Connaissance - the acquaintance.

But the aforementioned is no absolute truth...Some may refer to acquaintances as "mes amis" (my friends) as a generic term.

Mes copains/mes copines, mes potes doesn't necessarily mean one isn't referring to their best friends.

Calling a stranger "l'ami" usually denotes some irony.

In some parts of southern France, you might come accross people greeting each other by calling "collègue" (litterally meaning colleague but in this context "friend")

Last but not least, and that's where things get tricky, referring to your loved ones can be confusing :

Copain/copine is also the most commonly used word to refer to one's boyfriend/girlfriend (the older generations also tend to use ami/amie instead).

Petit copain/petite copine and petit ami/petite amie (litterally "little friend") is also a way to refer to your significant other.

It is all a matter of context and highly depends on your interlocutor. Good luck with french!

Best friend in French is meilleur ami

Sentences

Notre meilleur ami est médecin.

Our best friend is a doctor.

C'était mon meilleur ami au lycée.

He was my best friend in high school.

Je pense que tu es mon meilleur ami.

I look on you as my best friend., I think you're my best friend., I think you are my best friend.

Je suis votre meilleur ami.

I'm your best friend.

Il était mon meilleur ami.

He was my best friend.

Il était, est et sera mon meilleur ami.

He was, is, and will be, my best friend.

Tom est le meilleur ami de Marie.

Tom is Mary's best friend.

Il est le meilleur ami de mon mari.

He is my husband's best friend.

Je suis ton meilleur ami.

I'm your best friend.

Tu es m on meilleur ami.

You are my best friend., You're my best friend.

More Examples of Best friend in French

Je la considère comme ma meilleure amie.

I look at her as my best friend., I think of her as my closest friend.

Ma meilleure amie est à Rome en ce moment.

My best friend is in Rome now.

HOME IN FRENCH

French Words Describing the Home ('la Maison')

The home is the center of French family life, so words identifying the house, furniture, and areas of the home are a part of everyday language for French people. It's important, then, to learn some of the most common words for furniture, house, and home in French. Where provided, click the links to hear how the word is pronounced in French.

Ma Maison

Starting with maison (house), as well as chez moi (my home), several words describe a house in French, from searching for a home to buying your abode and perhaps renovating it.

la maison > house

chez moi > at my house, my home, at home

rénover, remettre à neuf > renovate, refurbish

construire, bâtir une maison > build a house

un architecte > architect

un agent immobilier > a real estate agent, house agent

acheter une maison > to buy a house

une perquisition domiciliaire > a house search

Inside la Maison

Once you're inside a French home, many French words describe its interior, from la cuisine (the kitchen) to le bureau (the office).

à l'intérieur > inside

architecte d'intérieur > interior designer

décorateur d'intérieur > home decorator

la pièce, la salle > room

la cuisine > kitchen

la salle à manger > dining room

le bureau > office, study

la salle de séjour, le salon > den, living room

la chambre, la chambre à coucher > bedroom

la salle de bain > bathroom (does not include a toilet)

la salle d'eau > shower room

les toilettes, les cabinets / le W-C (pronounced "vay say") > toilet / water closet (British)

la salle de jeu > playroom

une domestique, une femme de chambre > housemaid

le sous-sol > basement

le grenier > attic

la porte > door

le couloir > hall

un escalier > stairway

Furniture, Appliances, Equipment, and Home Furnishings

A number of words can discribe les meubles (the furniture) you might use to make your house a home.

les meubles > furniture

un meuble > a piece of furniture

le living > living room

mobilier design > designer furniture

des meubles en kit > self-assembly furniture

un bureau > desk

une imprimante > printer

un ordinateur > computer

ordinateur portable, PC (pronounced "pay say") portable > laptop computer

une étagère > bookshelf, shelving unit

une chaîne stéréo > stereo

une affiche > poster

une peinture > a painting

un canapé > couch

une chaise > chair

un rideau > curtain

une télévision, un télé, un TV (pronounced "tay vay") > television

une armoire, un placard > closet

un lit > bed

un oreiller > pillow

une commode > dresser

un réveil > alarm clock

un bain, une baignoire > bathtub

une douche > shower

un lavabo > bathroom sink

une toilette > toilet

une cuisinière > stove

un four > oven

un four à micro-ondes > microwave

un réfrigérateur > refrigerator

un évie > kitchen sink

une fenêtre > window

une lampe > lamp

une moquette > carpet

un tapis > rug

un miroir, une glace > mirror

un mur > wall

le parquet, le sol > floor

le plafond > ceiling

une porte > door

une table > table

un téléphone > telephone

Outside a Maison

Once you're comfortable with your home's interior, you might proceed à l'extérieur (outside), where you can use many words to describe the home in French.

à l'extérieur > outside

une garage > garage

la remise à calèches > carriage house/coach house

la maison d'invités > guest house

le porche, la véranda > porch, veranda

le balcon > balcony

le patio > patio

un auvent > an awning

une clôture > a fence

le pergola > a pergola (area covered with wooden timbers and climbing plants)

le jardin > yard, garden

un potager > a vegetable garden

un jardin de fleurs > a flower garden

un parterre > a flower bed

une jardinière > a flower box

une fontaine > a fountain

bain d'oiseau > a birdbath

jardinier > gardener

une allée > a driveway

une piscine en plein air / découverte > an outdoor swimming pool

le barbecue, le gril > an outdoor grill

TYPE

Appartement – flat/apartment

Chambres d'hôtes – guesthouse, B&B

Gîte – holiday cottage

Maison de maître – mansion or manor, usually in a town or village (literally 'master's house')

Maison de ville – town house

Manoir – manor, usually in the country

Maison de campagne – country house

Ferme, corps de ferme – farmhouse/farmstead

Fermette – small farmhouse

Bastide – large, detached stone house common in southern France

Longère – long, rectangular house common in Brittany and Normandy

Charentaise – stone house found throughout Poitou-Charentes

Maison à colombages – half-timbered house

Mas – large country house typically found in Provence

Château – French stately home, sometimes part of a wine-producing estate

Château fort – castle (fortified)

Domaine – estate

Vignoble – vineyard

Chaumière – thatched cottage

Pavillon – bungalow

Moulin – mill

Prieuré – priory

Pigeonnier – dovecote

Écurie – stable

Grange – barn

Atelier – workshop

Dépendance – outbuilding

Monument historique – listed building

For those unfamiliar with the language but interested in renting a French house or taking a step onto the property market, understanding what certain terms mean can become confusing for some buyers.

This guide will focus on the main types of property in France and how their appearance is defined. It will also concentrate initially on villas and the choices you have when coming to rent or buy. Whichever location appeals most to you, there are types of property and villas to suit everyone.

Villa d'architecte

The French refer to villas designed from the mid 20th century onwards as architect's villas. Their style, size, and design can vary from property to property meaning the choice will cater to the needs of various personal tastes. Contemporary villas can come in the form of smaller, one-storey attached houses and range up to large open buildings in sparse areas.

If a certain area of France appeals to you, such as the vibrant capital Paris or more rural southern regions, then looking into which villas are available in that location is advisable. For example, if you enjoy water-based activities then look for villas with pools or those located close to rivers, lakes or beaches.

The main reason for investing in a villa is to obtain a pleasant and relaxing residency to enjoy the delights of French scenery. Buying one is also a fantastic way to entertain a group of friends or relatives who choose to holiday in the country

Bastide

A 'bastide' name derives from medieval towns which were fortified during the 13th and 14th century, mainly located in the Aquitaine and Midi-Pyrénées regions. However, the name spread to classify other stone-build, detached houses further afield. They have practical layouts, square features and almost flat roofs which made them easier to construct. Different forms of 'bastides' have archways located on the ground level, making it possible to build verandas and garages as well.

A renowned example of a 'bastide' can be found in Villeneuve sur Lot, a town located in the southern Aquitaine region of France. Visitors will notice the Roman-grid arrangement of houses in the town which created an organised layout and helped officials collect taxes.

Charentaise

A Charentaise property is a traditional French house similar to a bastide in the way they are stone-made, rectangular in shape and have a practical layout. They commonly have one or two floors, with chimneys located at either end of the building. Although Charentaise houses are predominantly constructed from basic stone and wood materials, this doesn't mean to say they aren't fitted with all the mod cons to make living as comfortable as possible. Their name originates from the region the houses were initially built, Charente, which is one of the sunniest areas in France and easily accessible from the UK.

Domaine

A domaine is best defined as a property, or group of properties, that include a large plot of land also. Similar to an estate in England, where a house and its outbuildings are surrounded by woods and fields, a domaine is favourable for outdoorsy people. Interests such as caring for orchids and vineyards to pursuing tennis and hunting are trademarks of domaine properties.

Château

Château's are popular in France, ranging from very small dwellings to massive buildings with a whole host of rooms. The main selling point of a château is their cheap price to purchase, although some renovation and maintenance work can push the overall cost up. This is because they are generally very old buildings and the materials used to construct them need regular repairs.

However, if properly looked after then a château can become a fantastic investment for many English buyers. They offer a beautiful interior design along with scenic views, all to be enjoyed in the pleasure of substantial gardens. Numerous trees and stone-made walls are also a symbol of a château's outer lands.

Fermette/Longère

A fermette or longère is the equivalent of an English farmhouse, although they are usually much smaller in size. There are a number of these buildings dotted all over rural France, with similar stone features and quaint design. Investing in a fermette will usually entitle you to the surrounding lands and other outbuildings linked to the property, such as barns and sheds.

Maison à colombages

A Maison à colombages property is a timbered or wood-framed house. The framework is visibly made from strong wooden beams, often oak, with bricks, and clay usually making up the rest of the building. They are common in villages and hamlets in rural French regions, notably Alsace, and some people compare them to English Tudor architecture.

Maison de maître

The Maison de maitre converts into English as "master's house" and was constructed for wealthy businessmen or officials. It became a sign of prestige for the owner, displaying their status in the community. Their appearance is one of grandeur, with large windows and high ceilings. Maison de maitres will typically come with a well-designed garden and moderate plots of lands nearby.

Pavillon

Detached homes in France are known as pavillons, often found in the north of the country. The term mostly commonly refers to properties built from the mid 20th century onwards. Their extended size allows many of them to be fitted with a cellar and garage on the ground floor. Modern bungalows are sometimes referred to as pavillons also.

Overall, many English buyers look to the French property market due to the more appealing climate and the fact it isn't too far away. Travelling to any part of France is generally very simple. House prices are also commonly much less than their English counterparts and the strict property laws protect buyer's rights to a large extent.

French Property Law

My wife and I are considering buying a property in France. We both have children from a previous marriage. What things should we be considering when we buy?

There are two main issues you should consider - succession and inheritance tax. Many couples don't and end up incurring costs because they have to restructure their affairs so they can meet their objectives. Don't get swept along by fulfilling your dream of owning a property in France without considering these important points early on.

How you buy the property between you will dictate what will happen when one of you dies. Legal advice on your specific circumstances is recommended. Each case is different - it's not a matter of 'one size fits all'.

The first step is to identify who you want to own and have use of, the property on each death. You'd need to look at this in the round, taking into account how the rest of your estate is to be distributed on death. You should then consider whether you will be restricted by law in what you want to achieve.

French law will apply to the succession of the property on the death of an owner. Protected heirs (known as heritiers reservataires) have fixed inheritance rights to a minimum portion of your estate which is governed by French law. Protected heirs are usually your children. You may be surprised to know that a surviving spouse has only limited protection under French law. In some circumstances, other family members may have inheritance rights - but in your case, we are concerned about you, your wife and your children. There are two forms of joint outright ownership of the property - tontine and indivision. The default position is indivision in equal shares. If you want to reflect unequal contributions in the purchase deed, it's important to raise this with your legal adviser. If you own en indivision, on each of your deaths French law will dictate who is to inherit your portion of the property. For example, if you die before your wife, your children will have inheritance rights in respect of your share, leading to joint ownership with your wife. You'll need to think about whether this is likely to cause any problems for any of them. Might there be an issue if your wife remarries, wants to occupy the property permanently, wants to sell, or doesn't have a good relationship with your children? Also, would the divorce or financial difficulties of a child have an adverse impact on your wife's interest in the property?

Buying a property en tontine involves a system of automatic survivorship. It's a contractual arrangement between you whereby the last surviving owner is deemed to have been the sole owner from your purchase. This means that if you die before your wife, your children's inheritance rights are effectively overridden and the property passes into the sole ownership of your wife. You can only insert the tontine clause at the time of purchase so you must decide whether or not this option's for you before you buy.

It's important to understand the consequences of tontine ownership - particularly as it could lead to you disinheriting your children. Step-children have no statutory inheritance rights under French law in respect of a step-parent's estate so if you were to die before your wife and she becomes the sole owner of the property because you had a tontine clause, on your wife's subsequent death your own children will not be heritiers reservataires.

Your legal adviser should clarify all the consequences of tontine ownership and the circumstances in which an attack could be made on the tontine clause. For example, an argument could arise over the validity of the clause if you and your wife didn't make equal contributions to the purchase price, saying you have used the tontine clause to disguise a gift made from one to the other.

Another option is to sign a change of matrimonial property regime deed. You can have a system of community of assets (known as a communaute universelle) which has a similar effect to the tontine clause in that it gives automatic survivorship but would also apply to any future property purchased in France as well as the one you're intending to buy now. On your death, your wife would become the sole owner of the property. However, because your children are of a previous relationship they would have the opportunity to claim the portion of your estate that they would otherwise be entitled to under French law had you not signed the matrimonial property regime deed.

French succession law applies to the distribution of the French property on death because it is an immovable asset located in France. It's possible to change the asset in your estate to a movable asset, and assuming that you intend to retain your domicile of England and Wales (if this is your domicile) then English succession law would apply to the distribution of that asset - and allow you to distribute it to whoever you choose. You would buy the property through a company structure - for example via a French SCI (Societe Civile Immobiliere) - and each subscribes cash in return for a shareholding in the company which then uses the cash to buy the property. The asset in your estate is a shareholding which could avoid the application of French inheritance law but it won't avoid French inheritance law applying, though.Another option is to own the property in one name only - but you'd need to give careful thought to the consequences of doing this and whether it will achieve your objectives as to the distribution on the owner's death.

Once you've worked out the ownership option that best suit you, you'll need to think about how French inheritance tax law will apply.French inheritance tax is calculated by reference to your beneficiaries and the tax is payable by the beneficiaries rather than coming out of the estate. Each beneficiary has a nil rate band allowance and the amount depends on the relationship of the beneficiary to the deceased person. Your children will have a nil rate band allowance of 156,974 (all figures here are for 2010) where as stepchildren inheriting directly from you will only have an allowance of 1,570. The rate of tax for your children is calculated on a scale from 5% to 40%. A flat rate of 60% applies to stepchildren. It's essential to understand how the inheritance tax law will apply because you may be able to structure your affairs to minimise the tax bill for your beneficiaries.

There is a full exemption on transfers on death between spouses.

You should also think about your Wills at the time of purchase. If you don't have a Will covering the distribution of a French property then your wife would only be entitled to receive a one quarter share of your interest in the property. If it's covered by a Will you can increase the interest she gets by giving her a choice from a number of inheritance options, one is to take a life interest - an usufruit - over your share. This can be particularly helpful because it can give her exclusive occupation of the property while avoiding a 60% tax rate on a transfer from step-parent to stepchild - and it could help to achieve equality of inheritance of the property between the children (for example, if you each have two children.) It's essential to get advice on the pros and cons of taking an usufruit, though.

Although a Will in your home country may be recognised in France, it cannot override the application of French succession law and in many circumstances, it may be preferable to have a separate French Will.

FEELINGS AND EMOTIONAL STATES IN FRENCH

After this reading this book, you will be able to talk about your feelings in French. Being able to talk about your emotions in French will help you get to know people better and take your new friendships to the next level.

Phrases describing your emotions in French.

Je suis heureux(se).

I'm happy.

Je suis amoureux(se).

I'm in love.

Je m'ennuie.

I'm bored.

Je suis fatigué(e).

I'm tired.

Je suis impatient(e).

I'm excited.

J'ai peur.

I'm frightened.

Je suis en colère.

I'm angry.

Je me sens vivant(e).

I feel alive.

Je suis jaloux(se).

I'm jealous.

Je suis surpris(e).

I'm amazed.

Je suis content(e).

I'm content.

Je suis nerveux (se).

I'm nervous.

Je suis occupé(e).

I'm busy.

Je suis inquiet(e).

I'm worried.

Je suis furieux(se).

I'm furious.

Je suis surpris(e).

I'm surprised.

I'm embarrassed.

Je suis calme.

Je suis pressé(e).

I'm calm.

I'm in a hurry.

Je suis triste.

Je me sens bien.

I'm sad.

I feel balanced.

Je suis gêné(e).

EXPLAININGEMOTIONS IN FRENCH

L'esprit d'escalier

The phrase l'esprit d'escalier explains that irritating moment when you come up with the perfect witty comment or comeback, but the time has passed and it's too late. It translates as 'staircase wit' and has an interesting historical trajectory. It was reportedly invented by the 18th-century philosopher Diderot, who noted how he could only think of brilliant retorts after walking away from an argument, which was often down a flight of stairs.

L'appel du vide

Ever wonder what it would feel like to jump from a tall height? The French phrase l'appel du vide translates literally 'the call of the void', and refers to the peculiar urge to jump from high places. Standing at the top of the Eiffel Tower on a beautiful, sunny day in Paris with incredible views, has been known to fill awestruck tourists with this inexplicable feeling. Of course, it rarely leads to dangerous situations, though it does feel disturbing.

La douleur exquise

Since French is often thought of as the world's most romantic language (although perhaps the Italians would argue for that title!), there are many phrases relating to love. The phrase la douleur exquise is the 'exquisite pain' that one suffers from unrequited love. More than just physical discomfort, it sears right through the soul and have inspired artists and writers for centuries.

Empêchement

The French often say J'ai eu un empêchement. It is the perfect excuse for when you don't want to say exactly why you are late for an appointment; instead, you just had an 'unexpected last-minute change of plans'. The verb empêcher means to prevent, so this phrase hints at intentions being hindered by some unspecified and ambiguous force. It can be used if you're being secretive, but more often, it's just a lazy way to get out of having to explain yourself!

Sortable

There are certain family members and friends that you just know you can spend time with in public without fear of being shown up or embarrassed, but with others, it takes a little more forward-planning. In French, sortable is the adjective used to describe those people who you know won't ever embarrass you. It stems from the verb sortir which means to go out or exit, with sortable translating literally into someone you can take out.

Flâneur

The word flâneur (wanderer) originated in the 16th century, gaining a set of rich associations in the 19th century, thanks to French poet Charles Baudelaire. He crafted a portrait of the urban explorer so memorable – leisurely wandering the wide boulevards and cafés of the capital – that no picture of Paris is complete without it. The emotion it encapsulates is the idea of wandering with no particular goal, simply exploring for the pleasure of soaking up the atmosphere.

Râler

The French have worked up a bad reputation for their disgruntled habits over the years, especially Parisians, who have recently been labelled the biggest moaners in France. The word râler is the perfect way to describe someone whose behaviour is hovering unpleasantly between whining and complaining. The nuance arises from the fact that the French have actually developed it into a sophisticated art, expressing their dissatisfaction with the rest of the world!

Retrouvailles

In French, retrouvailles is one of the most heartwarming expressions. The word explains the happiness of meeting someone after a very long time, possibly after a long separation. You can say: on va fêter les retrouvailles to explain that you will be 'celebrating a reunion'; one that often takes places between lovers or loved ones and that can be very emotional. It stems from the verb retrouver which means 'to find again/rediscover'.

Frappadingue

One of the most amusing words in the French dictionary of words describing emotions that we can't explain relates to the explosive personality of your craziest friends. The word frappadingue is for someone who acts so crazy, perhaps spontaneously and dangerously, that it's like they've been hit on the head. The curious word is a hybrid blend of frapper (to hit) and dingue (crazy).

CHAPTER FOUR:
HUMAN BODY

Body Parts in French

The word for the body in French is le corps, but why stop there? Find out how to pronounce common body parts in French! I hope you don't need to use it, but you'll also learn how to say I'm sick in French – just in case!

Just as everything else in French, body parts are either feminine or masculine, which affects how you would describe them! Look at the following gender clues in both singular and plural forms:

Body parts in French

Le corps

The body

La jambe

The leg

Les jambes

The legs

La main

The hand

Les mains

The hands

Le pied

The foot

Les pieds

The feet

La tête

The head

Le ventre

The stomach

Le   dos

When a word begins with "Le", it means it falls into the masculine group of words, and when it begins with "La", it's feminine. Also, if the word is plural then it begins with "Les", no matter whether it is referring to a male or female gender word.

When describing physical pain, its useful to know a few expressions that might get you some help when you need it!

Mal

Pain or Ache

J'ai mal à la tête

I have a headache

J'ai mal au dos

I have backache

J'ai mal au ventre

I have a stomach ache

The Human Body Vocabulary

Front: forehead

Visage (masc.): face

Gorge (fém.): throat

Cerveau (masc.): Brain

Narine (fém.): nostril

Joue (fém.): cheek

Lèvre (fém.): lip

Machoire (fém.): jaw

Cheveu(x) (masc.) : hair

Barbe (fém.): beard

Moustache (fém.): moustache

Dent (fém.): tooth

THE BODY

Poignet (masc.) : wrist

Poing (masc.) : fist

Pouce (masc.) : thumb

Ongle (masc.) : nail

Cuisse (fém.) : thigh

Cheville (fém.) : ankle

Côte (fém.) : rib

Ventre (masc.) : belly, stomach

Estomac (masc.) : stomach

Dos (masc.) : back

Coeur (masc.) : heart

Foie (masc.) : liver

Poumon (masc.) : lung

Rein (masc.) : kidney

Sang (masc.) : blood

Nerf (masc.) : nerve

Os (masc.) : bone

Muscle (masc.) : muscle

Peau (fém.) : skin

The legs and lower body

les fesses (f) - the backside, buttocks

les jambes (f) - the legs

les cuisses (f) - the thighs

les genoux (m) - the knees

les chevilles (f) - the ankles

les talons (m) - the heels

les pieds (m) - the feet

les orteils (m) - the toes

The upper body

le dos - the back

les épaules (f) - the shoulders

la poitrine - the chest

les seins (m) - the breasts

les bras - the arms

les coudes (m) - the elbows

le ventre - the belly

les mains (f)

DIRECTIONS

If you travel to France, you might need help finding your way around. In this lesson, you will learn how to politely ask where a place is located and how to give directions.

Asking for Directions

Charlotte lives in Lyon but is visiting her cousins in Poitiers. She needs to mail a package and is trying to find la poste (pronounced: lah post), the post office. She looks around to see if she can find someone to ask: 'Où se trouve la poste?" (pronounced: ooh suh troohv lah post), meaning, 'Where is the post office?'

Charlotte is French, so it would never occur to her to just walk up to someone and ask where the post office is without first saying, 'Excusez-moi, monsieur' (pronounced: ex-kyooh-say mwah, muh-syeuh), which means, 'Excuse me, sir.' If speaking to a female, she would say, 'Excusez-moi, madame' (pronounced: ex-kyooh-say mwah, mah-dahm), meaning, 'Excuse me, ma'am.' She also follows her question with s'il vous plaît (pronounced: see vooh play), meaning, 'please.'

So, when Charlotte sees a woman, Madame Gauthier, outside a shop, she says, Excusez-moi, madame. Où se trouve la poste, s'il vous plaît?

Simple directions in French

Learning the left and right in French

The left La gauche

The right La droite

The book on the left Le livre sur la gauche

The bottle on the right La bouteille sur la droite

Turn left Tourne à gauche

Turn right Tourne à droite

The second right La deuxième à droite

The house to the left La maison vers la gauche

Compass directions

North: Le nord

South: Le sud

East: L'est

West: L'ouest

Forms of Directions

Take (A Street)

Madame Gauthier tells Charlotte to take Dubois Street, 'Prenez la rue Dubois' (pronounced: pren-ay lah rooh dooh-bwah). In France, most streets are rues, but you might also take le boulevard (pronounced: luh boohl-eh-var).

Cross (A Street Or Bridge)

Madame Gauthier explains that Charlotte will reach le pont (pronounced: luh pon), the bridge. She tells Charlotte, Traversez le pont (pronounced: trah-ver-say luh pon), meaning, 'Cross the bridge.'

Turn Left

Once across the bridge, Charlotte must turn left. Madame Gauthier tells her, Tournez à gauche (pronounced: toohr-nay ah gohsh).

Turn Right

Charlotte will come to Astérix Street. Madame Gauthier explains A la rue Astérix, tournez à droite (prounounced: ah lah rooh ah-stay-reeks, toohr-nay ah dwaht).

Major French Direction Words and Phrases...and How Do I Use Them?

Whether you're heading somewhere en bus (by bus), par train (by train), en voiture (by car) or à pied (by foot), it's crucial to know how to use the correct words and phrases.

Otherwise, how will you find anything, or, even more importantly, locate l'aéroport (the airport) or la gare (the train station) to begin your French journey?

Lock down these phrases before purchasing un billet (a ticket).

Tout droit

One of the most important direction phrases is tout droit, which means "straight ahead." Used in a sentence, it's often repeated a few times, sometimes with the tout repeated for emphasis:

"Oui, oui, juste tout tout droit." (Yes, just straight ahead.)

How it's used:

"Où sont les toilettes ?" (Where is the bathroom?)

"Il faut aller tout droit." (Go straight ahead.)

À droite

"To the right" is rather self-explanatory, but what gets tricky here is the pronunciation. It's imperative to note that droit in the direction phrase tout droit is pronounced /dʀwa/, while, due to the "e" at the end (indicating that you should pronounce all the letters in the word rather than cutting off the ending), droite should be pronounced /dʀwat/, with the "t" sound at the end. (For more information on the International Phonetic Alphabet and how to read it, visit their website).

As you first begin to use these direction words, pay special attention to this, as it's the difference between going straight and turning right. Three straights don't necessarily make a right!

How it's used:

"Excusez-moi, je cherche la boulangerie." (Excuse me, I'm looking for the bakery.)

"Si vous allez tout droit, puis à droite à la Rue Verte, elle est au coin de la rue." (If you go straight ahead, then take a right at the Rue Verte, it's at the corner.)

À gauche

There's no similar confusion on pronunciation here. À gauche simply means "to the left." Pronunciation is exactly like the word "gauche" in English—which means something completely different (lacking ease or grace).

How it's used:

"Où est le pont ?" (Where is the bridge?)

"Prenez à gauche au parc." (Take a left at the park.)

Nord, sud, ouest, est

The cardinal directions above (north, south, west, east) are useful in the city when you're familiar with the way the streets run and you know that Montmartre and the Sacre Coeur are north of the Louvre and the Tuileries.

A lot of locals will use the cardinal directions to tell you where to go, because, naturally, they're familiar with the city and how it's laid out.

Of course, if you're spending the day out hiking, these directions will be your only option—so either way, they're necessary!

How they're used:

"Est-ce qu'il y a un restaurant à côté ?" (Is there a restaurant close by?)

"Il y a un restaurant italien au sud de la gare." (There's an Italian restaurant south of the train station.)

Près de/à côté (de)

Just as important as knowing whether to turn right or left is identifying landmarks in relation to other landmarks. Près de, or "close to," along with à côté, is a phrase that will help you do just that.

Note that the preposition de contracts with le and les to make du and des respectively. This applies to the expressions above as well as to the other expressions in this post.

How it's used:

"L'église est près du métro." (The church is close to the metro.)

En face de

En face de (in front of) is another great direction word that will help you find your location while looking for landmarks and important places nearby.

How it's used:

"La maison est en face de l'église." (The house is in front of the church.)

Au coin de

This one's a bit more specific, but you might hear this phrase, meaning "at the corner of," in the city.

How it's used:

"Il y a un supermarché au coin de ma rue." (There's a supermarket on my street corner.)

How Do I Get to Paris? Ways to Ask for Directions

Où est

The simplest and quickest way to ask where something is located in French is to start the sentence with Où est... , or "Where is..."

Looking for the post office?

"Où est la poste ?"

The nearest coffee shop?

"Où est le café ?"

The library?

"Où est la bibliothèque ?"

It's quick, easy to pronounce and gets straight to the point.

Est-ce que

This structure will be useful when you're using basic question words like qui (who), quoi (what), quand/où (when), où (where) and comment (how), and really, when you're asking most questions.

Est-ce que functions as the "is/are/does" in a sentence like "Where is the church?" or "How does one get to Paris?"

For example:

"Où est-ce que je peux trouver la gare ?" (Where can I find the train station?)

"Comment est-ce qu'on peut aller au centre ville ?" (How can one get to the center of the city?)

Inverted subject-verb

One way to ask a question in French is to reverse the subject and verb and connect them with a hyphen. We do something similar in English.

For example:

"Puis-je aller au magasin ?" (Can I go to the store?)

This will come in handy when asking for directions, especially when you're wanting to avoid using the sometimes long-winded Est-ce que but still would like to be polite.

"Pouvez-vous me dire comment aller à Notre Dame ?" (Can you tell me how to get to Notre Dame?)

Appropriate Transition Words for Giving and Understanding Directions

Puis

Puis, or "then," is a simple transition word that is used when giving consecutive directions.

How it's used:

"Prenez à droite, puis allez tout droit." (Go right, then go straight ahead.)

Après

Après, or "after," has functionality similar to puis.

How it's used:

"Prenez à droite, et après, allez tout droit." (Go right, and after that, go straight ahead.)

Enfin

If you're receiving a set of directions that's particularly long, you may hear enfin, or "finally."

How it's used:

"Prenez à droite, puis allez tout droit, et, enfin, prenez à gauche au parc."

(Go right, then go straight ahead, and finally, take a left at the park.)

ANIMALS IN FRENCH

List of animal

Chêvre (fém.) : goat

Mouton (masc.) : sheep

Agneau (masc.) : lamb

Cochon (masc.) : pig, hog

Vache (fém.) : cow

Taureau (masc.) : bull

Veau (masc.) : calf

Lapin (masc.) : rabbit

Poule (fém.) : hen, chicken

Poussin (masc.) : chick

Coq (masc.) : cock, rooster

Canard (masc.) : duck

Dinde (fém.) : turkey

Oie (masc.) : goose

Mammals

• Cheval (masc.) : horse

• Poney (masc.) : pony

• Chat (masc.) : cat

• Chien (masc.) : dog

• Ours (masc.) : bear

• Sanglier (masc.) : boar

- Renard (masc.) : fow
- Cerf (masc.) : deer
- Écureuil (masc.) : squirrel
- Loup (masc.) : wolf
- Souris (masc.) : mouse
- Rat (masc.) : rat
- Chauve-souris (masc.) : bat
- Éléphant (masc.) : elephant
- Girafe (fém.) : giraffe
- Tigre (masc.) : tiger
- Lion (masc.) : lion
- Panthère (fém.) : panther
- Rhinocéros (masc.) : rhino
- Kangourou (masc.) : kangaroo
- Zèbre (masc.) : zebra
- Panda (masc.) : panda
- Guépard (masc.) : cheetah
- Jaguar (masc.) : jaguar
- Singe (small one) (masc.) : monkey
- Singe (big one) (masc.) : ape
- Chameau (masc.) : camel
- Hippopotame (masc.) : hippopotamus

Birds

Canari (masc.) : canary

Cygne (masc.) : swan

Hirondelle (masc.) : swallow

Alouette (masc.) : lark

Hibou (masc.) : owl

Autruche (fém.) : ostrich

Perroquet (masc.) : parrot

Aigle (masc.) : eagle

Faucon (masc.) : falcon

Insect

Abeiltle (fém.) : bee

Mouche (fém.) : fly

Moustique (masc.) : mosquito

Chenille (fém.) : caterpillar

Papillon (masc.) : butterfly

Cafard (masc.) : roach, cockroach

Ladybird (fém.) : coccinelle

Puce (fém.) : flea

Fourmi (fém.) : ant

Escargot (masc.) : snail

Ver (masc.) : worm

FISHES AND AQUATICS ANIMALS

Poissons et animaux aquatiques

Fish

Poisson rouge (masc.) : gold fish

Sardine (fém.) : sardine

Saumon (masc.) : salmon

Truite (fém.) : truite

Anguille (fém.) : eel

Anchois (masc.) : anchovy

Thon (masc.) : tuna

Méduse (fém.) : jellyfish

Requin (masc.) : shark

Baleine (fém.) : whale

Dauphin (masc.) : dolphin

Orque (masc.) : orca

Crabe (masc.) : crab

Coquillage (masc.) : shellfish

Homard (masc.) : lobster

Huître (fém.) : oyster

Moule (fém.) : mold

Pieuvre (fém.) : octopus

Pingouin (masc.) : pinguin

Reptiles (Reptils)

Serpent (masc.) : snake

Lézard (masc.) : lizard

Crocodile (masc.) : crocodile

Dinosaure (masc.) : dinosaure

Tortue (fém.) : turtle

Grenouille (fém.) : frog

Crapaud (masc.) : toad

ANIMALS DESCRIPTION IN FRENCH

Describing Exotic Animals

Nicole and her friend Jacques are at the zoo. They've walked past les flamants (flamingos), gawked at les phoques (seals), and they're now looking at les ours (bears). Nicole loves all the colorful and unusual animals at the zoo and can't wait to visit her favorite one next. But wait! She's forgotten what her favorite animal is called. Jacques tries to help by asking Nicole to describe what the animal looks like.

Nicole: Il est grand, et il a quatre pattes. (It is large, and it has four legs)

Jacques: L'éléphant?

Nicole: Non. Il a de la fourrure et des moustaches comme un chat. (No. It has fur and whiskers like a cat.)

Jacques: Le lion?

Nicole: Non. Il a des rayures noirs et oranges (No. It has black and orange stripes.)

Jacques: Le tigre?

Nicole: Oui! Le tigre!

Whether it comes to exotic animals at the zoo or your beloved pet, animals are a big part of our daily lives. Being able to describe animals is thus an important part of any language. In this lesson, we'll learn the names of some of the more common animals, as well as go over the basic components of describing animals, including physical characteristics like covering, patterns, and others.

Animal Names

Pets

In France, many people keep pets, and they often consider their animals to be a part of the family. Here's a list of common pets, known as les animaux domestiques (pronunciation: layz ah-nee-moh doh-meh-steek) in French, to help you, with the gender of the noun labeled as either masculine (m.) or feminine (f.):

Animal Translation Pronunciation

Animal	Translation	Pronunciation
cat	chat (m.)	shah
kitten	chaton (m.)	shah-tohn
dog	chien (m.)	she-ehn
puppy	chiot (m.)	she-oh
fish	poisson (m.)	pwah-sohn
parrot	perroquet (m.)	pehr-oh-kay
mouse	souris (f.)	soo-ree

On the Farm

If you're in a rural area, you might encounter a few farm animals. These are some of the most common animals you'd see at a farm in France:

Animal Translation Pronunciation

cow vache (f.)   vahsh

sheep mouton (m.) moo-tohn

pig cochon (m.)   koh-shohn

chicken poulet (m.) poo-lay

goat chèvre (f.)   sheh-vruh

horse cheval (m.)   shuh-vall

duck canard (m.)   kah-nar

Ocean Animals (Les Animaux Océaniques)

While you're studying things that are in or near the ocean, make sure to create bulletin boards and worksheets in French and English.

Dolphin - le dauphin Clam - la palourde (lah pah-loord)

Crab - le crabe (luh crahb)

Dolphin - le dauphin (luh do-fahn)

Eel - l'anguille (lohn-gee-uh) *Note the "g" is hard as in the first "g" in "garage."

Hermit crab - l'ermite (lehr-meet)

Jellyfish - la méduse (lah may-dooz)

Lobster - le homard (luh oh-mar)

Manatee - le lamantin (luh lah-mah-tahn)

Oyster - l'huître (luh-hwee-truh)

Pelican - le pélican (luh pay-lee-kahn)

Penguin - le pingouin (luh pehn-gwahn)

Polar bear - l'ours blanc (loors blah-unk)

Seahorse - l'hippocampe (leep-oh-kahmp)

Seal - le phoque (luh fawk)

Sea Lion - l'otarie (loh-tah-ree)

Shark - le requin (luh ri-kahn)

Starfish - l'étoile de mer (lay-twahl-duh-mare)

Stingray - la pastenague (lah pahs-ten-ah-gay)

Squid - le calamar (luh kal-ah-mahr)

Walrus - le morse (luh mohrs)

Whale - la baleine (lah bell-ehn)

Wild Animal

If you're like Nicole and Jacques and enjoy visiting the zoo, you'll probably need to know the names of your favorite animals, like the ones below. Luckily, many of these animal names are similar to their English counterparts, so they should be pretty easy to remember.

Animal Translation Pronunciation

lion lion (m.)   lee-ohn

tiger tigre (m.)   tee-gruh

elephant éléphant (m.) ay-lay-fohn

zebra zèbre (m.)   zeh-bruh

rhinoceros rhinocéros (m.) ree-noh-sayr-os

hippopotamus hippopotame (m.) ee-poh-poh-tahm

giraffe girafe (f.)   zhee-rahff

penguin manchot (m.) mahn-shoh

monkey singe (m.) sanzh

kangaroo kangourou (m.) kahn-goo-roo

Animal Characteristics

Now that you know the names of some common animals you may come across in someone's home, on the farm, or at the zoo, let's review some ways to describe the physical appearances of these animals.

Number of Legs

One of the first things you might notice about an animal is the number of legs it has. For most animals, you'll use the word patte (fem., pronunciation: paht) to refer to a leg, foot, or paw. Most animals have either two or four paws. Here are some examples:

L'autruche a deux pattes (The ostrich has two legs)

Le chat a quatre pattes (The cat has four legs/paws)

Le serpent n'a pas de pattes (The snake has no legs)

Tail

Many animals are also in possession of something that we humans lack: a tail. In French, the word for the tail is queue (fem., pronounced kuh). So, in action:

Le singe a une queue (The monkey has a tail)

L'araignée n'a pas de queue (The spider has no tail)

FOOD AND DRINK

History of France Food

Food is a very important part of life in France, which makes it also a very important part of French culture. While the British are known for afternoon tea and Americans are known for their bottomless buffets, the French embrace long, lingering meals that feature several courses. This food culture is integral to the dynamics of daily life in France.

A fast-paced, 21st century lifestyle has brought changes to France. For example, giant supermarkets that resemble major American chains have found their way to France in the last 20 years. While France was once the epitome of multiple-stop shopping (bread at the boulangerie, meat at the boucherie, cheese at the fromagerie, and vegetables from the outdoor market), more and more French shoppers are planning their meals by visiting the superstore hypermarchés every week.

Despite this trend, it is still very common for French people to buy the most important items (bread and pastries) from independent shops. While everyday meat is typically purchased at the supermarket, many families still visit the butcher to reserve a choice cut for special occasions. Likewise, many French citizens walk to the baker each morning to get a freshly baked baguette or round pain de campagne for the breakfast table.

What Do French People Eat

While meals in France tend to be long, breakfast can be a rather quick affair. While dinner and lunch may seem like long meals with an overabundance of food, breakfast may seem particularly limited by American standards.

French Breakfast

The French may reach for the coffee pot before the breakfast plate. While the default type of coffee in France is strong espresso (if you ask for un café in a restaurant, you will get an espresso), it is common to ask for a café au lait at breakfast. This coffee is served in a large, rounded bowl or mug, and has a lot of warm milk added to it. Less popular options are tea or hot chocolate. Some typical French breakfast alternatives to accompany that first cup of coffee are:

1. Baguette with butter: A piece of baguette with butter or jam is usually enough for a French breakfast.
2. Tartines: which is toast with jam, is loved for its simplicity and the sweet flavor that goes well with coffee.
3. Flaky: warm croissants are a popular breakfast item traditionally reserved for weekends, although less so these days. When in France, don't even think of eating one without having it warmed.
4. Pain au chocolat is a delicious, luxury morning pastry. On weekends, the rectangular chocolate-filled variant on a croissant is always a treat for the children. Sometimes, the bread/toast/croissants are accompanied by a bit of fresh fruit or plain yogurt.

French Lunch

You will find the most varied answers to what French people eat around the options available at lunchtime in France. Some French people abandon work for two hours to have a big meal served with wine. In urban centers, office workers may just grab a sandwich from a street vendor or from the takeaway display cases in a café.

Restaurant lunch: With this option, anything goes. A three- or four-course meal can consist of appetizer (salad, soup, or pâté), a meat or fish accompanied with a type of potato and a warm vegetable, followed by dessert and occasionally a cheese platter. This lunch is frequently served with wine. Of course, there are also restaurants serving lighter lunches with popular menu items.

Oysters on the half shell on ice are displayed in full view of passers-by. Products of the waters along the extensive coastline, the grade of oysters is important. Spéciale de Claire is better quality than Fine de Claire, and Spéciale Pousse en Claire is the best of all.

Salad Niçoise

Salade Niçoise

Salade Niçoise appears on many café menus. Named for the famous city on the French Riviera, tuna and hard boiled eggs are the proteins in this dish that also features boiled potatoes, tomatoes, Niçoise olives, capers, green beans, and sometimes, anchovies.

Soupe à l'Oignon Gratinée is never better than in France where it's a meal in itself. Fragrant and prepared to perfection with caramelized onions and a crusty lid of grilled gruyère (Swiss) cheese, French onion soup is a true classic.

Charcuterie is a selection of handmade sausages, air cured beef, dried ham, and pâté. Expect stone-ground Dijon mustard, cornichons and small pickled onions to accompany, along with baguette and cheese. Add a bottle of red wine... et voilà, you have a French picnic to share on a park bench.

Specialty crêpes restaurants and street vendors offer both the savoury and sweet varieties as the main meal or as a dessert.

Croque Monsieur is a not-too-distant relative of the American grilled cheese sandwich. It's an open face sandwich of baked ham and cheese crowned with a velvety béchamel sauce. Its variation is Croque Madame, which adds a fried egg on top.

French Dinner

Dinners in France vary depending on the day of the week, the season of the year, and how big of a meal lunch was. Couples who go home for a decadent lunch often have a simpler dinner whereas those who eat a sandwich at lunchtime might eat a larger dinner.

Because France is large enough to encompass a few very different climates and topographies, the main meal differs from north to south and from the Mediterranean to the Alps. For Sunday supper with extended family and on special occasions, dinners become longer, feature more courses (especially the cheese platter), and the dinner table is set out with quality linens, cutlery, serviettes, and plates. Someone announces "à table" when dinner is ready and everyone heads for their seats. If you're not a fan of steak or fish, try it in France, and you might well change your mind. Tempting, expertly made sauces are never far from reach.

For the famous bistro dish steak au frites, a lean entrecôte (ribeye) is grilled or pan fried, seared for a couple of minutes on each side and immediately served with a generous dollop of Roquefort or béarnaise flavored butter to melt on top of the meat. A mountain of crisp potato fries is obligatory, plus a simple green salad.

Fresh fish from the day's market, lightly grilled and served with potatoes and salad is another popular option.

Steamed Normandy mussels can be served with shallots and thyme in a white wine sauce for dipping slices of toasted baguette.

Bouillabaisse, originating in Marseilles on the Mediterranean Sea, is the classic French fish soup, a meal in itself.

Blanquette de veau, a creamy veal stew of white meat and white sauce, is the ultimate home-cooked meal and one of the most widely found dishes in France. It may be varied using lamb.

Slowly simmered chicken, Burgundy wine, mushrooms, onions, and bacon lardons are combined for heavenly coq au vin, an age-old French staple.

Boeuf Bourguignon, a sister dish to coq au vin, also hails from Burgundy and basically uses the same method with chunks of beef instead of chicken.

Cassoulet is a hearty one-pot meal originating in the southwest of France. The rich, slow-simmered casserole is a recipe built around meat (pork sausages, pork, goose, or duck) and white beans.

French fries

Lunch at home: Some French people still go home at lunchtime, and many of these people eat a warm meal, usually not as fancy as the multi-course restaurant meal. This practice is more common in the countryside, especially in outdoor jobs, where an escape from the midday sun offers a much needed break.

Street lunch: As work schedules get tighter and commutes get longer, particularly in urban centers, many more French people buy sandwiches on the street or in the train station at lunchtime. Popular sandwiches are on baguettes, with the most traditional choices being cheese or ham and cheese. You may also be able to find boiled eggs, tuna, and salami.

French Cuisine

While there is no specific daily French diet, there are plenty of foods that are typical in French houses and restaurants. Coffee and wine are closely linked to the food culture as well. Visitors to France will appreciate the fine food as well as the simple, fresh ingredients.

CELEBRATIONS

France has many national celebrations and shares some of these with the rest of the world. Holidays like Christmas, Easter, Halloween, and Eid are all celebrated. However, France has its own twist on these celebrations and has its own national festivals such as Bastille Day and May Day. Bank holidays are not set on a Friday or a Monday and if they fall on a Thursday or a Tuesday, for example, it is not uncommon for employers to offer their employees the opportunity to "faire le pont" (make a bridge) to get a longer weekend by taking extra days off. There are also many regional festivals.

Why celebration such as Bastille Day celebrated?

France's major national celebration is Bastille Day on 14th July. This is to celebrate the French Revolution which established the way France functions today. La Bastille was a prison in Paris, which the revolutionaries stormed to free prisoners on 14th July 1789. Today, it is celebrated as a national holiday with fireworks and parades. There are also lots of French flags on display, as this flag was introduced as a symbol of the new republic.

May Day

On 1st May, France celebrates May Day. This is also celebrated around the world as a traditional spring holiday. It is also international Labour Day, which is a day to celebrate workers' rights. In France, the lily of the valley has become a symbol of the day and a good luck charm. This dates back to 1561 when King Charles IX gave all the ladies in his court a lily of the valley.

common celebration

Christmas - Noël

Joyeux noël – Merry Christmas

Bonne année – Happy new year

Much like the UK and around the world, many people in France also celebrate Christmas. It is a time for getting together with family and friends and sharing gifts.

Christmas celebrations

France also has La Fête des Lumières (lights) on 8th December in Lyon when the city puts on a huge light show. Everyone around the city joins in lighting candles and lighting their houses to make the city glow. There is also La Fête des Rois (epiphany) which is celebrated on the first Sunday after 1st January and is also an important holiday in the Christmas season.

Christmas food

After Midnight Mass on Christmas Eve, people gather at home or in a restaurant for a feast called le réveillon.

This usually consists of oysters (les huîtres), snails (les escargots), seafood (les fruits de mer), smoked salmon (le saumon fumé), foie gras or caviar as a starter, followed by goose (l'oie) or some other roasted bird for the main course, accompanied by wine (le vin) or champagne (le champagne). Each region in France has its own traditional menu, with dishes like goose, chicken, turkey, chestnuts, and oysters. Some typical French Christmas foods include:

le boudin blanc - a white sausage made of pork

la bûche de noël (yule log) - a log-shaped cake made of chocolate and chestnuts

le pain calendal (in southern France) - Christmas loaf

treize desserts (in Provence) - a series of 13 desserts

aigo-boulido - garlic soup

la brouillade de truffes - omelet with truffles

les papillottes - chocolate treats

la Galette des Rois (on Epiphany) - a round cake which is cut into pieces and distributed by a child, known as le petit roi or 'enfant soleil hiding under the table. Whoever finds a fève- the charm hidden inside - is King or Queen and can choose a partner.

Christmas presents - Les cadeaux de noël

In some parts of France, Christmas comes early when Father Christmas brings small gifts and sweets for children on 6th December, the feast day of Saint-Nicolas (celebrated in the North and Northeast).

French children leave out shoes instead of stockings for Santa. Santa Claus is known as le père noël, (aka papa noël). Children place their shoes by the fire and wake up on Christmas Day to find them filled with presents from Father Christmas and fruit, nuts and small toys hanging on the tree. Christmas Day is mainly a day of celebration for children. There is also le père fouettard (Papa Whipper) who gives out punishments for naughty children.

While the French open their Christmas presents (les cadeaux de noël) on this day or on December 24th though, not all parents do – they wait until New Year's Eve, la Saint-Sylvestre, which is an adult celebration.

Christmas decorations

Le sapin de noël - the Christmas tree is the main decoration. It first appeared in Alsace region in the 14th century and became a mainstay across France in the 19th century.

La crèche de noël – a nativity scene with santons (figurines), which are displayed in churches and many homes.

Le gui - mistletoe is hung above the door during the Christmas season to bring good fortune throughout the year.

Easter celebrations - Pâques

Easter and lent are big celebrations in France and lent is preceded by the famous Mardi Gras festival which is celebrated around the world. Easter Fish is the French equivalent of April Fool's Day, taking place on 1st April. It is a tradition that children create paper fish, pinning them to unsuspecting adults and while saying Poisson d'Avril (April fool).

Mardi Gras

Mardi Gras translates as 'Fat Tuesday'. It is a big celebration and feast before the start of lent (traditionally a period of fasting before Easter). The festival has Christian as well as non-religious origins. It is a carnival with people dressing in colourful costumes. In New Orleans in the USA, Mardi Gras has become a major world famous celebration.

Nice Carnival-Nice Carnival

Québec, the French-speaking area of Canada, is famous for its Winter Carnival which consists of sports events, a masquerade ball, and banquets.

Ice castle at Québec Winter Carnival.Ice castle at Québec Winter Carnival

The Winter Carnival in Quebec

Crêpe Day (La chandeleur)

Crêpe day is on the 2nd of February. Crêpes are similar to pancakes. The festival is also called la chandeleur (the festival of light). It is similar to Pancake Day in the UK, in that the main activity is to eat pancakes (des crêpes).

HOLIDAYS THAT BRINGS CELEBRATION

In France, we know how to celebrate life on many occasions! Whether you are visiting Paris or the Province, holidays and celebrations in France will definitely bring an 'exotic taste' to your stay. Did you know that the French annual calendar is punctuated with eleven bank holidays? As well as a number of religious, civil and commemorative celebrations? I hope this book will give you some insights about what to expect on your next travel to France!

Holidays and Celebrations in France Holidays and celebrations in France play an integral part of the country's popular culture.

Public Holidays in France

The French observe 11 official public holidays, five (5) of them are civil holidays:

New Year's Day (Jour de l'An),

May Day (1er Mai or Fête du Travail),

Victory in Europe Day (Armistice du 8 mai 1945),

Bastille Day (Fête Nationale), and

WWI Armistice Day (Armistice du 11 novembre 1918).

Public holidays have a religious origin based on the Catholic faith: Easter Monday (lundi de Pâques),

Ascension Day (Jeudi de l'Ascension),

Whit Monday (Lundi de Pentecôte),

Assumption Day (Assomption),

All Saints' Day (Toussaint), and Christmas (Noël).

In addition, people living in the two départements of Bas-Rhin and Haut-Rhin in Alsace and in the Lorraine département of Moselle enjoy two additional public holidays:

124

Good Friday (Vendredi Saint), and St. Stephen's Day (Saint-Etienne – known as Boxing Day in English-speaking countries).

This is due to historical reasons when the three départements were returned to France in 1918. Celebrations in France Every season has its share of celebrations and festivals.

Epiphany (Epiphanie)

Candlemas (Chandeleur)

Mardi-Gras & Carnivals (Carnaval)

Valentine's Day (Saint-Valentin)

April Fools' Day (1er avril)

Europe's Day (Journée de l'Europe)

Mothers' Day (Fête des Mères)

Fathers' Day (Fête des Pères)

World Music Day (Fête de la Musique)

HOLIDAY AND CELEBRATION

Holidays and Celebrations in France: local events Some celebrations in France are local events, including sporting events. A few examples: Lemon Festival in Menton (Fête du citron de Menton) Easter Feria of Arles Festival of Avignon International Kite Festival of Berck-sur-Mer Transhumance Festival in Saint-Rémy-de-Provence Roland Garros French Open in Paris Rouen Armada Deauville American Film Festival Cannes Film Festival Tour de France cyclist race Grande Braderie of Lille Mondial Air Ballons festival in Lorraine Inter-celtic Festival of Lorient European Heritage Days (Journées européennes du patrimoine) Return from the alpine pastures (Fête des Alpages) Wine harvest festivals in Alsace Christmas market of Strasbourg (Marché de Noël de Strasbourg) Saint-Nicolas celebrations in Nancy Foire aux Santons in Marseille Festival of Lights in Lyon (Fête des Lumières de Lyon)

School Holidays in France School holidays (les vacances d'été) play an important part in the tourism industry in France. The dates are set by the Ministry of Education (Ministère de l'Éducation nationale). They vary depending on the zones the schools are located. There are three school zones in France. They are not contiguous in order to facilitate access to sports resorts and tourist sites. Therefore, the winter and spring holidays don't take place at the same time whether a school is based in Paris, Strasbourg or Toulouse. Thus relieving the pressure on skiing and Mediterranean resorts.

Periods of holidays The French school calendar includes five periods of holidays: The Summer holidays are the longest and the most awaited by pupils and teachers. The two-month break starts at the beginning of July and ends early September. Autumn holidays or All Saints holidays (les vacances d'automne or de la Toussaint) last two weeks around the beginning of November. Christmas holidays (les vacances de Noël or de fin d'année) last two weeks and include Christmas and New Year's Day. Winter holidays (les vacances d'hiver) are two weeks long and take place between the second week of February and the first week of March. Spring holidays (les vacances de printemps or de Pâques) do not always encompass Easter. They take place between the second week of April and the first week of May.

Holidays and Celebrations in France: the Four Seasons France is situated in the Northern Hemisphere. As its fellow European neighbouring nations, it goes through a cycle of four distinctive seasons: Spring – le printemps Summer – l'été Autumn – l'automne Winter – l'hiver

GOING OUT AND PARTYING

Places to Party in France

With all its famous attractions, it can be easy to forget that it's also that France has got a fantastic nightlife. top 5 places to party in France.

Marseille

Arriving in the Southern port city of Marseille is like arriving in another country- the natives speak French but they consider themselves to be "Marseillais". There city has a history stretching back 2,600 years and has amassed a great deal of diversity over this time; around one quarter of the population have North African roots and there are also strong influences from West Africa and Italy. This diversity has helped shaped Marseille's colourful nightlife. A lot of the centrally located clubs and bars are in Vieux Port. The area really captures the culture of Marseille and is home to the sports bar Le Canebière, and the famous Bar de la Marine, which was used in the 1930s film Marius. The cost of a pint is about £6.

Paris

The capital of France is a great place to catch the train in Europe as it has connections throughout the continent, it's also a great place to stop for a party. While there is a sense of quantity over quality, among a lot of the tacky and soulless bars and clubs there are some real gems, including the Batofar, which is a club set on a boat on the Seine. The club has a strong urban influence and has helped a lot of new urban music to breakout in the city. If you travel to France looking for pure Parisian extravagance, however, there is La Perle, which has trendy clubbers, trendy music, and trendy, inflated prices, the cost of a pint here is significantly higher than the city average of £6.

Bordeaux

Bordeaux is the capital of one of France's biggest wine regions, however, while it may be more famous for the scholarly side of getting hammered, it still has lots of places to let your hair down in. Despite being one of the most exclusive places in France, the large student population in the area helps to keep the cost of a pint down to around £4.20. A popular student haunt is Sénéchal, a club with strong 70s overtones. Le Lucifer is also great fun; it serves 250 different types of beer from around the world and has live rock music on Wednesdays.

Le Havre

In the northwest of France is the vibrant port city of Le Havre. The city was devastated in the second world war but has overcome this difficult period in its history to become a fun and exciting place, particularly at night. It is situated along the coast of the English Channel and is a great place to go out if you're headed down south from Calais. The bars and clubs in Le Havre offer an interesting mix of expensive clubs and pubs as well as those that suit a tighter budget. An average cost of a pint in the city is around £4.

Strasbourg

The beautiful architecture in the city of Strasbourg is incorporated into its fun, student oriented nightlife. It is this young clientele that helps to keep the nightlife in Strasbourg so fun and cheap, with an average pint costing under £4. The area's nightlife is also heavily influenced by a strong Germanic culture. The city has historically been passed between Germany and France and is a great place to experience the best of both cultures simultaneously. The Académie de la Bière is open daily until 0400 and serves 70 different types of beers, while Le Chalet is a fun club with two dance floors, a great mix of people and karaoke.

QUESTION AND ANSWER

French Questions

This series of French lessons on questions will cover all that you need to know to be able to ask (and respond to) the questions that you will most commonly use in France and other French speaking countries.

Asking Questions in French

This lesson covers the 4 key ways to ask questions in French. Luckily, they are very similar to the English ways of asking questions! Not only that, get loads of audio examples of each type and really get to grips with asking questions in French.

"How are you?" in French

When you meet French people it's important to get off on the right foot using the correct terminology. This lesson shows you the correct way to say How are you? in French for both formal and casual situations.

Parlez-vous français?

A very common French phrase is Parlez-vous français? This is a phrase you can expect to be asked whenever you encounter French-speaking people at home or abroad. There are several variations of Parlez-vous français ? that can be used, so check out this lesson to expand your knowledge!

French for "What is your name?"

Another common French phrase that you will often encounter is someone asking you "What is your name?" in French. In fact, you may well use it yourself as an ice-breaker of sorts. In this lesso, we also find out a few more phrases to keep the conversational ball rolling.

Using "When?" in French

Digging a little deeper into one of the common interrogative words, this lesson shows you plenty of examples of how to use "When?" in French. For example, it could be very handy to know the French phrase for "When does the flight leave?"!

"Where?" in French

In our final lesson on French questions, we cover the all important interrogative word, "Where?" in French. This is particularly important when asking for directions, and we cover a couple of other ways to ask the same thing in a different way.

TRAVELLING

Even if you don't speak much French, some of the best basic vocabularies you can have are related to transit. This lesson should help you to get around and to have a good time when you get where you're going. Before getting into specific vocabulary, however, here are some basic questions that you might find handy:

À quelle heure part...? (ah kell ör par) / At what time does ... leave?

C'est par où...? (say par oo) / Which way is ...?

On cherchait ... (ohn shehr-shay) / How do I get to ...?

Literally, 'On cherchait' means 'One was looking for'; this impersonal construction is the most polite way to ask for directions.

En Route

Planes

You probably won't be spending much time in airports, but just in case:

L'avion (lah-vee-ohn) / airplane

L'aéroport (ly-roh-por) / airport

La carte d'embarquement (lah kart dehn-bar-kö-mehn) / boarding pass

La livraison de bagages (lah lee-vray-zohn dö bah-gahzh) / baggage claim

La douane (lah doo-ah-nn) / customs

Le vol (lö vol) / flight

La compagnie aérienne (lah cohn-pah-nyee ah-ay-ree-en) / airline

In the unlikely event that you're in an airport without monolingual signs, you shouldn't have any trouble identifying les arrivées (layz-ah-ree-vay) as 'arrivals' and 'les départs' (lay day-par) as 'departures.' Carry-on luggage is a bit less intuitive, though: French just says 'les bagages à main.'

Trains

If you're visiting France, trains are a great way to get around between cities, even if you're not taking one of the famous high-speed trains, popularly known by their moniker, TGV (tay zhay vay). Arrivals and departures are, of course, the same for trains as for airplanes. Here's some other useful vocabulary:

La gare (lah gar) / train station

Le quai (lö kay) / platform

Le train (lö trahn) / train

Le guichet (lö ghee-shay) / ticket counter

En retard (awn rö-tar) / late

If you're waiting for a train at the station, you might ask if a train is delayed: 'Est-ce que le train pour Rouen est en retard?' If listening for an announcement (either in the station or on a train) you might hear a different construction: 'Le train arrivera avec dix minutes de retard,' the train will arrive ten minutes late.

Automobiles

If you're going to small towns (or just don't want to be tied to train schedules), you'll want an automobile. Here's some vocabulary you'll want 'sur la route' (sür lah root), on the road.

La voiture (lah vwahtür) / car

Le volant (lö vohlawn) / steering wheel

Le clignotant (lö klee-nyoh-tawn) / turn signal, or indicator

French Travel Phrases Guide

Have a little time before traveling? Then try to immerse yourself in French while at home, to give yourself a little practice. Pay a visit to FluentU's French video library and familiarize yourself with the tones and sounds of French, as well as the vocabulary you'll need to communicate smoothly while abroad. We've tracked down a great assortment of real-world French videos to help speed along your learning process with French for travelers as well as general French.For a quick but thorough guided experience in conversational French learning before you board your plane, try ed2go's Beginning Conversational French to get a foothold on the language. This course covers French for practical scenarios, exactly the kind you're bound to encounter while strolling around abroad.

1. Bonjour. S'il vous plaît... (Hello, please...)

Of all the common French phrases you could learn, don't miss this one. Whenever you're planning on asking anyone in France anything, from directions to how much something in a store costs to whether menus are available in English, always start with "Bonjour. S'il vous plaît..."The combination translates directly to "Hello, please..." but imagine it as just one phrase so that it's always at the beginning of your sentences.

While saying "please" might seem like a no-brainer, "bonjour" is actually just as important in French culture.

The way that Americans are able to walk into a store and ask for something without saying hello first is astounding in France, though it doesn't seem to bother many people Stateside. Neglecting to greet people is a surefire way to make the locals gruff and grumpy in their responses. So always remember this handy phrase. If you use it, no matter how many mistakes you make further down the line while speaking, your interlocutor will be more willing to help or make the effort to understand. All of the following sentences (aside from number two!) require this one as an opener—don't forget!

2. Oui/Non (Yes/No)

"Yes" and "no" in French can be very useful when trying to attempt basic communication with a French person. Once they realize you're mainly using French for travelers and don't have too much vocabulary to form your own sentences, they might make take charge of the interaction by asking you questions.Oui and non can always be useful to answer these questions and hopefully reach a helpful conclusion. You can make it more polite by tacking on merci (thank you)—as in, "oui, merci" or "non, merci."

3. Parlez-vous anglais? (Do you speak English?)

While it's nice to be able to ask all of your questions in French, if you really need to speak English, this is the key to unlock that possibility. A lot of French people do speak basic English, especially in big cities like Paris.Tourists who report that nobody in France speaks English were probably some not-so-savvy travelers who ran up to the first people they saw and started babbling in English without even a bonjour. This is seen as very rude in French and rarely gets the desired response.

On the other hand, if you ask someone to use their English skills—nicely, politely and in French—even someone who knows just a handful of words in English will likely want to try them out. With basic French, you already know and their basic English, you'll probably be able to communicate enough to get the job done.

4. Où est-ce que je peux trouver un plan de la ville? (Where can I find a city map?)

One of the first things you should get your hands on when visiting a new city if you haven't brought one with you is a map.

You'll find one at most tourist offices, but you can also buy them in shops.

This question will also help if you're looking for a map posted within the city. You'll find them fairly frequently in Paris. If you ask a local, they might be able to direct you to the nearest one.

As these maps are usually only of the nearby area, they can be particularly helpful if you're looking for directions to somewhere that you know is nearby but can't seem to locate. You'll be able to take a look at the smaller streets that might not appear on larger maps of the whole city.

5. Je cherche le bus/train/métro. Où est l'arrêt le plus près? (I am looking for the bus/train/subway. Where is the nearest stop?)It can be tricky trying to move around in an unfamiliar city. Sometimes having a map just isn't enough.

It's always good to know some French phrases for public transit so that you can ask people how to get to important destinations. The best thing to do in most French cities, particularly in Paris, is to find the closest bus (bus), train (train) or métro (metro) stop. Not only will you be able to get to where you need to be much more easily, but most stops in France have a map posted outside of them.

This will help you see where exactly you are in relation to where you need to go.

6. Où est...? (Where is...?)

Où est is an extremely useful and adaptable French phrase.

If you're looking for something else that isn't a map or bus stop, use this phrase to ask "Where is..." Finish it with whatever you're looking for: la Tour Eiffel, Notre Dame, le Louvre, but also un café (a café), un restaurant (a restaurant), un parc (a park), un supermarché (a supermarket) or une pharmacie (a pharmacy).

If you're looking for les toilettes publique (public toilets), however, you may be out of luck. Public toilets can be difficult to find in France—although in Paris you'll find some on the streets near touristy spots and you can even use this map of public toilets around the Paris metro system.

Otherwise, your best bet is to order in a café and use their bathrooms. You'll pay about a euro or two for the coffee, but the toilets will be clean.

7. Où est le guichet? (Where is the ticket window?)

One of the first steps to visiting a tourist spot in France is buying a ticket. If you're looking for the ticket window, ask for the guichet. You'll soon be ready to visit the museum, gallery, landmark or another site.

This useful French phrase will also be helpful if you're buying any other sort of ticket, from a movie ticket to a train ticket to a metro ticket. Anywhere you need to purchase an entry or access pass of any kind will have a guichet, and you'll need to find it to take full advantage.

8. Combien ça coûte? (How much does it cost?)

Here's another very useful and multifaceted French travel phrase. It can work nearly everywhere: in a store when you'd like to buy an item, on the bus or at the museum ticket window.

However, if you're looking to pay your bill in French restaurants, stick with "L'addition, s'il vous plaît," which will get you the bill, not a price.Food culture is so important in France that food idioms color the entire language. This is why it's especially important to be aware of restaurant etiquette while in France.Asking the price of a menu item is usually seen as rude, as prices are posted on the menu. There is some cultural context to restaurant price visibility. Prices will be posted when you're meant to see them, and they will not be posted when you're not meant to see them. For example, in old-school fancy gourmet restaurants, menus with prices may not be given to the ladies at the table.

9. Non, merci. Je regarde pour l'instant. (No thank you. I'm just looking for now.)

French service is not the same as American service. The overly friendly waiters you'll find in American restaurants are nowhere to be found, but salespeople might seem a bit aggressive or over-eager to Americans visiting France. The reason is simple: especially in fancier shops, salespeople are seen as experts. They want to help you find what you need. If you're just browsing, the above sentence can come in handy. When you do need their help, be sure to let them know! If you're excited about getting into the French shopping scene, learn all the essential French phrases you'll need to hit the boutiques.

10. Où est l'ambassade américaine? (Where is the American Embassy?)

Travel French isn't just about getting around, eating well and having fun. There are also French phrases to know in case of an emergency.

If you run into trouble in France, one good address to have on hand is that of the American embassy (ambassade). A stolen U.S. passport or ID card can be replaced at the embassy, and you might need their help if there is ever a political problem in France and you need to exit the country quickly.

That's a rarity to be sure, but it's better to be prepared while traveling!

11. J'ai une assurance voyageur. (I have traveler's insurance.)

If you're sick or injured and need to see a doctor, you might be asked about your assurance (insurance). If you have a traveler's insurance—as well you should!—this is how you can let someone know.

12. J'ai besoin d'aide. Je me sens menacé. (I need help. I feel threatened.)

If you feel scared for any reason, this sentence is sure to help. It's vague enough that you can use it even if you just suspect you're being followed or feel uneasy. It's also grave enough that if you've been attacked or threatened, you can get the police to you very quickly.

13. Merci beaucoup! (Thank you very much!)

Whenever you're done with any interaction, be sure to thank the person for their help by saying merci beaucoup! This sentence makes sure that the interaction ends on a pleasant note.

14. Excusez-moi – "Excuse me."

To get someone's attention, whether they're a waiter in a restaurant or a stranger on the street, say "excusez-moi", "excuse me".

This is also a polite way to ask someone to get out of your way. For example, if you're trying to exit a crowded train, a soft "excusez-moi" should (hopefully) be enough to make people step aside.

15. Pardon – "Sorry"

Once you've escaped that crowded train, be careful you don't bump into anyone as you walk through the crowded metro station. But if a collision does occur, it's fine. Just say pardon, "sorry", and all will be forgiven.

"Pardon?" is also how you'd ask someone to repeat themselves if you didn't hear or understand what they said. In this case, you should say it with a rising tone to indicate that it's a question.

Another way to say this is "pourriez-vous répéter, s'il vous plaît?" – "could you repeat, please?"

16. Je ne comprends pas – "I don't understand"

Sometimes pardon doesn't quite cut it. If you really can't figure out what the other person is saying, try telling them "je ne comprends pas" – "I don't understand."

There's no shame in being a beginner! Just remember not to fall back to English when the going gets tough. If you don't understand something, persevere in French anyway – it's the only way you'll learn.

10. Que veut dire ça? – "What does that mean?"

Maybe the reason you didn't understand is that there was a specific word you didn't recognise. If that's the case, say "que veut dire X?" – "What does X mean?"

You can also phrase this as "ça veut dire quoi?" – "what does that mean?"

11. Plus lentement – "More slowly"

Sometimes, vocabulary isn't the problem. You'd know the words if you could make them out, but you can't because the other person is talking too damn fast! In this case, try saying plus lentement – "more slowly". Better yet, say a full sentence: "Pourriez-vous parler plus lentement, s'il vous plaît?" – "Can you speak more slowly, please?"

12. Comment dit-on __ en français? – "How do you say __ in French?"

What if you need to say something in French, but the exact word escapes you? Just fill in the blank in the above sentence: "Comment dit-on X en français?" means "how do you say X in French"?

A side note: the pronoun on, seen above, is an interesting one. It's a colloquial alternative to nous ("we"). However, on is also used to refer to an unspecified person or people in general, like the word "one" is sometimes used in formal English. (If you speak German, note that on in this sense is like the German word man.)

One doesn't use the word "one" very much in modern English – one finds it rather old-timey and stuffy. These days you normally use "you" when you're talking about people in general.

13. Comment ça s'écrit? – "How do you spell that?"

If you learn a new French word using the phrase above, you might want to write it down before you forget it.

Unfortunately, French spelling isn't the easiest. The relationship between spelling and pronunciation is very complicated. Generally, it's easier to figure out a word's pronunciation from its spelling than it is to know its spelling from its pronunciation.

So if you're not sure, ask someone "comment ça s'ecrit?" – "how do you spell that", literally "how does that write itself?"Or if you don't trust your own transcription abilities, try asking them to write it for you: say est-ce que vous pouvez l'écrire? – "can you write it (down)?"

14. Où est...? – "Where is...?"

Struggling to find your way around? Not to worry. Just get a stranger's attention (remember, what phrase would you use to do this?) and ask "où est X" – "where is X?"

"X" could be many things: la Tour Eiffel, le Louvre, Notre Dame... or perhaps something less exotic, like le metro or un restaurant.

15. Où se trouve la station de métro la plus proche? – "Where is the closest metro station?"

Another way of saying "where is it?" is où se trouve, literally "where is (it) found". Here's an example of où se trouve combined with another handy phrase to know: la station de métro la plus proche means "the closest metro station".

One more piece of useful vocabulary: once you're in the the metro station, you might want to ask someone "où est le guichet?" = "Where is the ticket window?"

16. Je voudrais acheter un billet – "I would like to buy a ticket"

Now that you've found the guichet, you probably want to buy a billet – a ticket. But what type of ticket do you want?

un billet aller simple – a one-way ticket

un billet aller retour – a round-trip ticket

Make your decision, and tell the assistant "je voudrais un billet aller simple/retour pour X" – "I would like to buy a one-way/round-trip ticket to X", where X is your destination.

17. C'est combien? – "How much is it?"

France isn't the cheapest of countries – so whether you're at the guichet or elsewhere; it doesn't hurt to be price-conscious.

To ask how much something costs, say "c'est combien?" – "how much is it?" You can also say "Combien ça coûte?" – literally, "how much does it cost?"

18. Où sont les toilettes? – "Where are the toilets?"

It's worth learning this phrase because you might need it in a hurry! Où sont les toilettes mean "where are the toilets?"

Although if you want to use a public toilet, you could be searching for a long time. They aren't very common in France – and if you do find one, you'll probably have to pay to use it. You're probably better off buying something in a café and using their toilets instead.(Why is it "où sont", when previously we used "où est"? Easy: sont means "are" while est means "is". Since toilettes are plural, you must use sont, not est – "where are the toilets?", rather than "where are the toilets", which wouldn't make sense.)

19. À quelle heure est-ce qu'il faut régler la note? – "What time is check out?"

If you're checking into a hotel in a French-speaking country, one useful thing to know the checkout time. One way to find this out is to ask "à quelle heure est-ce qu'il faut régler la note?" – "What time must we check out?"- Another equivalent expression is: "quelle est l'heure limite d'occupation?"

20. La carte/le menu, s'il vous plaît. – "The menu, please."

France is famous for its food, so while you're there, you'll probably want to dine in a restaurant or two!

When dining out in any language, there are usually a few subtleties around how to order. Here I'll explain one of the more important things to know in French: the words for "menu".

I say "words" because there are two main ways to say "menu" in French.

The general word is carte, which you may recognise from the expression à la carte.

A carte is what you typically think of when you hear the word "menu". It's a list of individually-priced options; you pick and choose what you want, then add up the prices to get your total bill.But you can also ask for a menu, which is usually called a "fixed-price menu" in English. When ordering from a menu, you pick an option for each course (starter, main course, etc.) and pay the same, fixed price no matter what you selected.Whichever option you choose, inform the serveur/serveuse (waiter/waitress) by saying "la carte/le menu, s'il vous plaît" – "the menu/fixed-price menu, please."

21. Je ne peux pas manger... – "I can't eat..."

This doesn't apply to everybody, but for those to whom it does apply, it's very important: informing the waiter about your dietary restrictions. The simplest way to do this is to say "je ne

142

peux pas manger X" – "I can't eat X". Here are some of the more common ways to fill in the blank:

les cacahuètes – peanuts

les noix – nuts

le gluten – gluten

les fruits de mer – shell fish

les œufs – eggs

le poisson – fish

les produits laitiers – dairy products

le soja – soy

la viande – meat

If you're vegetarian, say so with "je suis végétarien" (for men) or "végétarienne" (for women.)

SET PHRASES,MODISMS,IDIOMATIC
EXPRESSIONS

Do you know how to say "an apple a day keeps the doctor away" in French? What about "to split hairs?" Learning the French translations for popular expressions and idioms is a great way to study French and add to your vocabulary.As you browse through this list, you will find many popular English expressions translated into French. Not all of them, however, are direct translations. Instead, they were translated in order to make sense in French, not to be a word-for-word meaning.

For instance, the phrase être aux cent coups are used to express that someone "doesn't know which way to turn" (that they're making a choice). Yet, if you place the French phrase into an online translator like Google Translate, you get the result of "to be a hundred shots." That is far from the intended meaning, which is why computers are not your best source of translation.

Human translators use the same logic employed by those who created these words of wisdom. You will use the same logic when translating and this is why it is important to continue studying French rather than rely on computers. Have fun with these expressions and allow this lesson to influence your own translations. Since you're familiar with the meaning of the expressions, it should be a little easier to grasp them in French.

A Bird in the Hand Is Worth Two in the Bush

An English phrase, "a bird in the hand is worth two in the bush" means that it is best to be happy with what you have rather than be greedy and ask for more.

In French, the phrase translates to Un chien vivant vaut mieux qu'un lion mort. Along with that same thought, you might encounter someone who likes to dwell on things, complain, or make too much of something. In that case, you may choose to use one of these phrases:

Chercher la petite bête > to split hairs (look for something to complain about)

Laisser quelqu'un mijoter dans son jus > to let someone stew in his own juices

Monter quelque chose en épingle > to blow something all out of proportion

Caught Between a Rock and a Hard Place

Many cultures express a similar sentiment, though the phrase "caught between a rock and a hard place" is thought to originate in the United States. It speaks to the tough decisions we often have to make in life.

The French translation is Entre l'arbre et l'écorce il ne faut pas mettre le doigt.

Decisions are difficult and sometimes you "don't know which way to turn." Fortunately, there are two ways to express that in French.

"To not know which way to turn":

Ne pas savoir où donner de la tête

Etre aux cent coups

Of course, you may make a choice that seemed like a good idea but didn't end up as well as you planned. Someone may remind you that:

L'enfer est pavé de bonnes intentions. > The road to hell is paved with good intentions.

However, there is always an optimistic approach and the ability "to see the light at the end of the tunnel" (voir le bout du tunnel). Or, you can try "to see life through rose-colored glasses" (voir la vie en rose).

To Always Have Your Head in the Clouds

Sometimes you meet dreamers who may seem "to always have one's head in the clouds." This phrase dates back to the 1600s and has English roots.

In French, you might say: Always have your head in the clouds.

Often, those people are only looking for direction in their life or have lofty ambitions:

Search saddle way > to search for one's path in life

Castles in Spain > to build castles in the air

Of course, just the opposite may be true and you might encounter someone who is simply lazy. A popular French phrase for that is Avoir hair in la main a. The literal translation is "to have a hair in the hand," but it is understood as "to be lazy."

There are other ways to say the same sentiment in a more direct manner:

Il ne s'est pas cassé la tête. (inf) > He didn't overtax himself (put any effort into it).

Il ne s'est pas cassé le cul. (slang) > He didn't bust his butt.

Il ne s'est pas cassé le tronc. (fam) > He didn't do much (try very hard).

Il ne s'est pas cassé la nénette. (fam) > He didn't do much (try very hard).

Leave the Best for Last

You want to end something with a bang, right? It leaves a lasting impression and is a little reward to remember and enjoy. That is why we love the phrase "to leave the best for last."

The French would say: Laisser le meilleur pour la fin.

Or, they might use one of these phrases, which are more along the lines of "to save the best for last":

Garder le meilleur pour la fin

Garder quelqu'un pour la bonne bouche

Now, you might want "to kill two birds with one stone" (faire d'une pierre deux coups) while completing a list of tasks. And when you get near the end, you can say "It's in the bag" (C'est dans la poche).

On Its Last Legs

If you would like to use the old adage "on its last legs," you can use the French phrase en bout de course, which can also be used to mean "ultimately."

Yet, there is more than one way to relay that someone or something is wearing out:

À bout de course > on its/one's last legs

À bout de souffle > breathless, out of breath; on its last legs

It's not always the end, though because "where there's a will, there's a way" (quand on veut, on peut).

You might also want to use these popular idioms for motivation:

Aux grands maux les grands remèdes. > Desperate times, desperate measures; Big problems require big solutions.

Battre le fer pendant qu'il est chaud > to strike while the iron is hot

That Costs an Arm and a Leg

Money is a popular subject for words of wisdom and one of the most popular was reportedly coined in America after World War II. Times were tough and if the cost was high, someone might have said, "That costs an arm and a leg."

Translating that to French, you might say: Ça coûte les yeux de la tête. (literally, 'an arm and a head)

You might also have been forced "to pay through the nose" (acheter qqch à prix d'or) or been deceived in the value of something "to buy a pig in a poke" (acheter chat en poche).

And yet, we all know that "time is money" and that is true in any language, including French: Le temps c'est de l'argent.

It's also best to use your money wisely and these two proverbs remind us of that:

Bonne renommée vaut mieux que ceinture dorée. > A good name is better than riches.

Les bons comptes font les bons amis. > Don't let money squabbles ruin a friendship.

Like Father, Like Son

The popular idiom, "like father, like son" alludes to the question of how nature and nurture lead to the people we become.

In French, the translation for this phrase (also meaning "like breeds like") is Bon chien chasse de race.

To put it plainly, you might also say "He's a younger version of his father" (C'est son père en plus jeune).

That's not as fun and there are other French phrases you might want to choose instead:

Les petits ruisseaux font les grandes rivières. > Tall oaks from little acorns grow.

Les chiens ne font pas des chats. > The apple doesn't fall far from the tree.

C'est au pied du mur qu'on voit le maçon. > The tree is known by its fruit.

When the Cat's Away, the Mice Will Play

When the person in charge leaves, everyone is free to do as they please. It happens with school children and even adults at work and that is why we say "when the cat's away, the mice will play."

If you wanted to say that phrase in French, use on of these:

Le chat parti, les souris dansent.

Quand le chat n'est pas là les souris dansent.

It might also be that someone is playing around and said "to be up to one's old tricks again" (faire encore des siennes). They may also get into trouble and are said: "to sow one's wild oats" (faire ses quatre cents coups).

Hopefully, they are not "like a bull in a china shop" (comme un chien dans un jeu de quilles). But, then again, "a rolling stone gathers no moss" (pierre qui roule n'amasse pas mousse). So one old-fashioned proverb may just cancel out another because it's okay to be playful. Right?

In the Morning of One's Life

Age is a popular subject for idioms and proverbs and two of our favorites speak about the young and not-so-young.

Au matin de sa vie > to be in the morning of one's life

Au soir de sa vie > to be in the evening of his life

That's much better than saying 'young' and 'old,' now isn't it? Of course, you can have a bit of fun with:

Avoir quarante ans bien sonnés (inf) > to be on the wrong side of 40

And yet, no matter your age, "you have all the time in the world" (vous avez tout votre temps) which can also mean "all the time you need." That's a great way to look at life.You might also meet or admire those special people in the world who are said: "to be a man/woman of his/her time" (être de son temps).

Every Cloud Has a Silver Lining

Optimists love the phrase "every cloud has a silver lining" and it sounds beautiful either way you choose to translate it into French:

À quelque-chose malheur est bon.

Après la pluie le beau temps.

Sometimes things get a bit challenging and you "can't see the forest for the trees" (l'arbre cache souvent la forêt). But if you look at it another way, it's possible that "it's a blessing in disguise" (c'est un bien pour un mal).

And many times you just have to sit back, let things go, and enjoy life:

Il faut laisser faire le temps. > Let things take/follow their (natural) course.

Laisser vivre > to live for the day, to take each day as it comes

On the Tip of My Tongue

When you can't quite remember something you might say that it's "on the tip of my tongue." If you're learning French, this is probably happening a lot.

To express this in French use: Avoir sur le bout de la langue.

You can always say, "Hang on, I'm thinking" (Attends, je cherche).

Hopefully, you don't fall victim to this malady, because it can be a bear to get rid of:

Avoir un chat dans la gorge > to have a frog in one's throat

Grinning From Ear to Ear

When you are delighted about something, you may be said "to be grinning from ear to ear" because you're wearing your biggest smile.

In French, you would say Avoir la bouche fendue jusqu'aux oreilles.

Someone may feel like this because the are said "to be free to do as one pleases" (voir le champ libre) and that is a good feeling.

Of course, one can always choose "to change for the better" (changer en mieux) if things aren't going quite right. Or, they might choose "to give the green light, or the go-ahead" (donner le feu vert à) to do something new.

That Sends Shivers up My Spine

Every now and then, you want to say, "That sends shivers up my spine" when something happens that frightens you or gives you the creeps.

There are two ways to say this in French:

Ça me donne des frissons. > That sends shivers up my spine.

Ça me fait froid dans le dos. > That gives me the shivers.

Then again, we all have things that annoy us and you can let someone else know with one of these phrases:

Ça me prend la tête! > That drives me crazy!

C'est ma bête noire. > It's my pet peeve.

It's as Easy as Pie

The idiom "it's as easy as pie" doesn't refer to baking a pie, but eating it. Now, that is easy!

If you'd like to say this in French, use: C'est facile comme tout (or, it's a breeze)

For a more literal translation of another idiom, try "c'est entré comme dans du beurre" (it's like a knife through butter).Or, you can take the easy way out and simply say, "It's easy" (C'est facile). But that's no fun, so here are two more idioms:

C'est plus facile à dire qu'à faire. > Easier said than done.

Paris ne s'est pas fait en un jour. > Rome wasn't built in a day.

Lucky at Cards, Unlucky in Love

Luck and love, they do not always go hand-in-hand and the old phrase "lucky at cards, unlucky in love" explains that well.

If you want to say this in French: Heureux au jeu, malheureux en amour.

You might, on the other hand, have "a stroke of luck" in love, in which case, you can say one of these lines:

Coup de pot (fam)

Coup de veine (inf)

Some people, however, prefer to "leave nothing to chance" (il ne faut rien laisser au hasard).

Beggars Can't be Choosers

Dating back to the 1540s, the expression "beggars can't be choosers" is a popular line to pull on someone who doesn't like what they are given.

If you would like to relay this concept in French, you have two options:

Nécessité fait loi.

Faute de grives, on mange des merles.

Of course, you might also wish to remind them that sometimes you have to take what you can get "for lack of anything better" (une faute de mieux).

And, you have to appreciate these words of wisdom:

Ne mets pas tous tes oeufs dans le même panier. > Don't put all your eggs in one basket.

Qui trop embrasse mal étreint. > He who grasps at too much loses everything.

Clothes Don't Make the Person

There are those people who try very hard to impress anyone and everyone and that is when you might use the old-fashioned expression, "Clothes don't make the person."

In French, you would say L'habit ne fait pas le moine.

If you would like to speak in plain terms, try these sentences which both mean "he's/it's nothing special" or "nothing to get excited about."

Il ne casse pas trois pattes à un canard.

Il ne casse rien.

Speaking of outward appearances, you might like to pull out this old phrase to speak about someone who's trying to cover up who he really is:

Qui naît poule aime à caqueter. > A leopard can't change his spots.

Then again, they may just be following the crowd, because:

Qui se ressemble s'assemble. > Birds of a feather flock together.

He Always Has to Put His Two Cents In

The conversation is fun and sometimes it can be a challenge, particularly when you're speaking to a know-it-all. You might say "He always has to put his two cents in."- Translating that into French: Il faut toujours qu'il ramène sa fraise. (familiar)

Sometimes you just can't get it (do you feel like that in French sometimes?) and you want to say, "It's all Greek to me" (J'y perds mon latin).

If you learn those two expressions, then you cannot miss these:

Mon petit doigt me l'a dit. > A little bird told me.

Ne tourne pas autour du pot! > Don't beat around the bush!

Don't Put the Cart Before the Horse

When someone's doing something completely backward, you might dig up the old adage, "Don't put the cart before the horse." Think about it, it makes sense!

In French, you would rattle off the sentence: Il ne faut jamais mettre la charrue avant les boeufs.

It's also important to not jump to conclusions and you might advise someone, "don't judge a book by its cover" (Il ne faut pas juger les gens sur la mine).

Old expressions love chickens and eggs. Here are two more pieces of sage wisdom:

Il ne faut pas vendre la peau de l'ours avant de l'avoir tué. > Don't count your chickens before they're hatched.

On ne fait pas d'omelette sans casser des oeufs. > You can't make an omelet without breaking eggs.

An Apple a Day Keeps the Doctor Away

Can we have a discussion about famous expressions without including "an apple a day keeps the doctor away?" No, we cannot.

If you would like to translate this into French, tackle this sentence: Il vaut mieux aller au moulin qu'au médecin.

We'll finish off with a simple list of some of our favorite old-time expressions, which will never go out of style:

Il vaut mieux être marteau qu'enclume. > It's better to be a hammer than a nail.

Il vaut mieux s'adresser à Dieu qu'à ses saints. > It's better to talk to the organ-grinder than the monkey.

Aide-toi, le ciel t'aidera. > Heaven helps those who help themselves.

Au royaume des aveugles les borgnes sont rois. > In the kingdom of the blind the one-eyed man is king.

Avec des si et des mais, on mettrait Paris dans une bouteille. > If ifs and ands were pots and pans there'd be no work for tinkers' hands.

C'est la poule qui chante qui a fait l'oeuf. > The guilty dog barks the loudest.

Ce sont les tonneaux vides qui font le plus de bruit. > Empty vessels make the most noise.

À l'impossible nul n'est tenu. > No one is bound to do the impossible.

À l'oeuvre on reconnaît l'artisan. > You can tell an artist by his handiwork.

À mauvais ouvrier point de bons outils. > A bad workman blames his tools.

The shoemakers are always the most badly shod. > The shoemaker always goes barefoot.

Literal meaning: "To lose your ball"

What it really means: To lose your head

"Ce n'est pas la mer à boire"

Literal meaning: "It's not like you have to drink the ocean"

What it really means: It's not difficult

"Faire la grasse matinée"

Literal meaning: "To have a fat morning"

What it really means: To sleep in

"Passer une nuit blanche"

Literal meaning: "To have a white night"

What it really means: To stay up / awake all night (usually on purpose, not because of insomnia)

"Passer un mauvais quart d'heure"

Literal meaning: "To have a bad quarter of an hour"

What it really means: A short, difficult period in one's life

"Dormir à la belle étoile"

Literal meaning: "To sleep in the pretty star"

What it really means: To sleep outside

"Être blanc comme neige"

Literal meaning: "To be as white as snow"

What it really means: To be completely innocent

"Faire boule de neige"

Literal meaning: "To make like a ball of snow"

What it really means: To get bigger / more important

"Faire du chemin / faire son chemin"

Literal meaning: "To go along the path / to go along your path"

What it really means: To make progress

"Mordre la poussière"

Literal meaning: "To bite the dust"

What it really means: To suffer a defeat

"Traîner quelqu'un dans la boue"

Literal meaning: "To drag someone through the mud"

What it really means: To dirty someone's reputation

"Se perdre les chèvres"

Literal meaning: "To lose your goats"

PROVERB AND SAYING

1. À vaillant coeur rien d'impossible. -Jacques Cœur

"For a valiant heart, nothing is impossible."

2. Dans une grande âme tout est grand. -Blaise Pascal

"In a great mind, everything is great."

3. Chacun voit midi à sa porte. -French proverb

"Everyone sees noon at his own door."

4. Je pense, donc je suis. -Rene Descartes

"I think; therefore, I am."

5. On ne change pas une équipe qui gagne. -French proverb

"One does not change a winning team." In other words, if it ain't broke, don't fix it.

6. Prouver que j'ai raison serait accorder que je puis avoir tort. -Pierre Augustin Caron de Beaumarchais

"Proving that I am right would be admitting that I could be wrong."

7. On n'est point toujours une bête pour l'avoir été quelquefois. -Denis Diderot

"Being a fool sometimes does not make one a fool all the time."

8. Il n'y a pas de verités moyennes. -Georges Bernanos

"There are no half-truths."

9. Chassez le naturel, il revient au galop. -French proverb

"Chase away the natural and it returns at a gallop," is very similar to the English saying about leopard and their spots.

10. Il vaut mieux prévenir que guérir. -French proverb

"It is better to prevent than to heal."

11. Le temps est un grand maître, dit-on. Le malheur est qui'il tue ses élèves. -Hector Berlioz

"We say that time is a great teacher. It's too bad that it kills all its students."

12. Être adulte, c'est être seul. -Jean Rostand

"To be an adult is to be alone."

13. Un homme seul est toujours en mauvaise compagnie. -Paul Valéry

"A lone man is always in poor company."

14. A vaincre sans peril, on triomphe sans gloire. -Pierre Corneille

"To win without risk is a triumph without glory."

15. L'enfer, c'est les autres. -Jean-Paul Sartre

"Hell is other people."

16. La raison c'est la folie du plus fort. La raison du moins fort c'est de la folie. -Eugène Ionesco

"Reason is the madness of the strongest. The reason for those less strong is madness."

17. Autres temps, autres mœurs. -French proverb

"Other times, other customs."

18. La vérité vaut bien qu'on passe quelques années sans la trouver. -Jules Renard

19. Il faut bonne mémoire après au'on a menti. -Pierre Corneille

"A liar should have a good memory."

20. Qui craint de souffrir, il souffre déjà de ce qu'il craint. -La Fontaine

"He who fears suffering is already suffering that which he fears."

21. Il vaut mieux faire que dire. -Alfred de Musset

"Doing is better than saying."

22. La parfaite valeur est de faire sans témoin ce qu'on serait capable de faire devant tout le monde. -La Rochefoucauld

"True valor is to do in secrecy what you could just have easily done before others."

23. La vies est une fleur dont l'amour est le miel. -Victor Hugo

"Life is a flower of which love is the honey."

24. Il n'y a qu'un bonheur dans la vie, c'est d'aimer et d'être aimé. -George Sand

"There is only one happiness in life, to love and be loved."

25. Aimer, ce n'est pas se regarder l'un l'autre, c'est regarder ensemble dans la même direction. -Antoine de Saint-Exupery

"Love doesn't mean gazing at each other, but looking, together, in the same direction."

26. Choisissez votre femme par l'oreille bien plus que par les yeux. -French proverb

"Choose a wife rather by your ear than your eye."

27. Plus l'offenseur m'est cher, plus je ressens l'injure. -Jean Racine

"The more dearly I hold the offender, the more strongly I feel the insult."

28. Va, je ne te hais point. -Pierre Corneille

"Go, I don't hate you."

29. On n'aime que ce qu'on ne possède pas tout entier. -Marcel Proust

"We love only what we do not wholly possess."

30. L'amour est comme le vent, nous ne savons pas d'où il vient. -Honoré de Balzac

"Love is like the wind, we never know where it will come from."

31. La vies est un sommeil, l'amour en est le rêve. -Alfred de Musset

"Life is a long sleep and love is its dream."

32. Le cœur a ses raisons que la raison ne connaît pas. -Blaise Pascal

"The heart has its reasons which reason knows nothing of."

33. Le seul vrai langage au monde est un baiser. -Alfred de Musset

"The only true language in the world is a kiss."

34. Entre deux cœurs qui s'aiment, nul besoin de paroles. -Marceline Desbordes-Valmore

"Two hearts in love need no words."

35. Vivre sans aimer n'est pas proprement vivre. -Molière

"To live without loving is to not really live."

Short French Quote

36. Oh! Si tu pouvais lire dans mon coeur, tu verrais la place où je t'ai mise! -Gustave Flaubert

"If you could read my heart, you would see the place I have given you there."

37. L'amour c'est être stupide ensemble. -Paul Valéry

"Love is being stupid together."

38. Un seul être vous manque et tout est dépeuplé. -Alphonse de Lamartine

"Sometimes, only one person is missing, and the whole world seems depopulated."

39. C'est cela l'amour, tout donner, tout sacrifier sans espoir de retour. -Albert Camus

"That is love, to give away everything, to sacrifice everything, without the slightest desire to get anything in return."

40. L'amour est une passion qui ne se soumet à rien, et à qui au contraire, toutes choses se soumettent. -Madeleine de Scudéry

"Love is a passion which surrenders to nothing, but to the contrary, everything surrenders to love."

41. Le prix d'Amour, c'est seulement Amour... Il faut aimer si l'on veut etre aimé... –Honoré d'Urfé

"The price of love is love itself. One must love if one wants to be loved..."

42. On ne voit bien qu'avec le coeur. -Antoine de Saint-Exupery

"We see well only with the heart."

43. Un peuple malheureux fait les grands artistes. -Alfred de Musset

"An unhappy nation makes great artists."

44. L'œuvre d'art, c'est une idée qu'on exagére. -André Gide

A work of art is an idea that someone exaggerates."

45. Les livres sont des amis froids et sûrs. -Victor Hugo

"Books are cold and certain friends."

46. Le monde est un livre dont chaque pas nous ouvre une page. -Alphonse de Lamartine

"The world is a book – with each step we open a page."

47. Ècrire, c'est une façon de parler sans être interrompu. -Jules Renard

"Writing is a way to talk without being interrupted."

48. Imaginer c'est choisir. -Jean Giono

"To imagine is to choose."

CPSIA information can be obtained
at www.ICGtesting.com
Printed in the USA
BVHW072310290321
603633BV00002B/264